Loose the Captive

Loose the Captive
Finding A Life Worth Living

Deanna L. Miller

Xulon Press Elite

Xulon Press Elite
2301 Lucien Way #415
Maitland, FL 32751
407.339.4217
www.xulonpress.com

Unless otherwise indicated, Scripture quotations taken from Scripture quotations taken from the New King James Version (NKJV). Copyright © 1982 by Thomas Nelson, Inc. Used by permission. All rights reserved.

Edited by Xulon Press

Printed in the United States of America.

ISBN-13: 978-1-54560-733-6

Contents

Foreword vii

Introduction. 1

Most Important Day of My Life 5

Processing What Just Happened 23

Control 28

Yielding. 33

Anger. 37

Suicidal Thoughts. 43

Dissociative Behavior. 52

Cross-dressing Years. 57

Nature vs. Nurture 63

Expectation of Rejection. 67

Repressed Memories 71

Lesson Learned from Cupcake 81

What Could Have Been 85

Conclusion. 91

References 99

About the Author 101

Foreword

What is the worst thing you have ever been through in your life? Does it still haunt you? Or have you tucked it away and convinced yourself it is not important? Have you forgotten about it completely? Anyone who has experienced deep suffering knows full well how the darkness and hopelessness can so easily overtake and consume you. Pain has a certain way of forcing us to look in the mirror at the raw image staring back at us. It challenges and sometimes even shapes our identity.

I would venture to say that all of us have faced this type of earth-shattering pain, and in our innermost being have heard our despairing cries for help. Some of us desperately grasp at the material things around us to dull the ache within, while others latch on to relationships so tightly in hopes of being saved. As a Licensed Professional Counselor and trauma specialist, this is where I spend the majority of my time: sojourning with people as they walk through their deepest, darkest pain.

When I first met Deanna, she briefed me on her story and identified her counseling goal: to work through her traumas. Like many of the individuals with whom I work, I noticed that her narrative contained a lot of facts without much emotion. In regards to the traumatic parts of her life story, she seemed very disconnected from herself. I greatly enjoyed her sense of humor and wit—an amazing characteristic for someone who has been through so much (and a characteristic she integrates throughout her book). Yet I still wondered: where was her emotional connection to her story? I knew that deep within Deanna there was a part of her that needed to be freed. I also felt that as she began working through her traumas with EMDR therapy and faced her deepest wounds in a way she never had before, God would meet her there.

My time working with Deanna was truly a treasure. I am continually amazed by her courage and her desire to see her story provide hope and encouragement to others who feel completely helpless and trapped in life. It takes some guts to battle PTSD symptoms and share your story of childhood abuse, becoming transgendered, and then being "untransgendered" in a confidential setting with a counselor. And it takes some *serious* guts to take that a step further and share it with the world! It is a joy to see that Deanna is now not only giving the facts of her story, but sharing and expressing her emotions as she tells it.

This book is Deanna's story … well, part of it. How could any of us ever put to words both the hardest and the most joyful things we have experienced? And of course, nobody could truly capture every detail of their life by pen! The words she has written on the following pages tell her narrative of how God rescued her from utter despair and redeemed her suffering for His glory.

In many ways, Deanna's story is our story. Granted we have not all experienced sexual, physical, and emotional abuse, nor have we all wrestled with gender identity issues. But like Deanna, we have *all* experienced the shame and depravity resulting from the brokenness within this world and the brokenness within one another. And, like Deanna, we all respond by looking for someone who can rescue and redeem us, something greater than this world has to offer.

Deanna's story is God's story. He sees the pain that permeates our souls and longs to rescue us out of the miry pit. He desires to comfort us, to heal us, to draw us closer to Him. He has done this for Deanna, and He will do it for you if you give Him permission.

Through Christ, healing *is* possible. Just as Deanna has reached a place of peace despite everything she has been through, so can you.

I invite you to keep an open mind as you read the words on the following pages. Deanna's book will likely confront you with your fears, challenge you to see a different perspective, and encourage you to reflect on how we relate to one another as humans. I often tell my clients that I wish they could have my job for a day. When it comes down to it, we are all struggling human beings. We all need to be understood and loved unconditionally, and we all need a Savior. Yet what most of us see is the façade of everyone else who "has it all together." It is my hope that as you read Deanna's book, you will realize that you are not beyond hope. It's okay to not have it all together. We are all works in progress, and you always have access to a Heavenly Sojourner in Jesus Christ.

Lauren Queen, MA, LPC, LCPC, NCC
Licensed Professional Counselor (Missouri)
Licensed Clinical Professional Counselor (Illinois)
National Certified Counselor
EMDRIA Certified

Introduction

have spent many days and nights thinking about sharing my life story. Where does the story begin? What needs to be shared, and what doesn't? Would anyone else benefit from hearing what I went through? Those questions were always with me, never ceasing, and almost taunting me. I began to believe that I should share it all — everything I have experienced. It is humbling to think that any of my experiences would help another. On the other hand, I know how much I had to yield to God's work to allow myself to be healed.

I have also wondered where to start my story. Should I write about everything that I endured as a child? I am not writing my story to get your sympathy. Everything that happened to me has made me into the person I am today. I do not seek to justify my many unhealthy behaviors, nor try to explain the actions of others in my life. Each and every event that occurred shaped my life into where it was when I accepted Jesus Christ as my personal Savior. This is where I choose to start my story. After all, this is when my life really began.

Deciding to follow Christ was the first of many steps needed to find the healing that is promised to us in the Gospel. Isaiah 53 holds my favorite verses that I held onto throughout my journey. Below I have used the New King James version to share, however I urge you to read it in the Amplified and The Message.[1] In those versions, the words are different, with the meaning being the same.

However, it will give pause to think about all that was freely given to each one of us.

Surely He has borne our griefs
And carried our sorrows;
Yet we esteemed Him stricken,
Smitten by God, and afflicted.
But He *was* wounded for our transgressions,
He was bruised for our iniquities;
The chastisement for our peace *was* upon Him,
And by His stripes we are healed.

An incredible price was paid so that we may walk in freedom. It is a wonderful thing to realize that Jesus is the Son of God and we all need Him. Why stop there? Why miss the last sentence? Chastisement, His beating, the rebuke that He withstood was for our peace. Peace: freedom of the mind from annoyance, distraction, anxiety, an obsession; to have tranquility and serenity. To be healed — doesn't that sound enticing? To be free from the war that battles inside, to gain understanding about why you do what you do that you know you shouldn't do. To overcome all that wears you down, that frustrates you about yourself. Simply put, to be whole. Whole could be defined a plethora of ways: Free from deficiency. Complete. Or possessing or being in a state of health and soundness.

The story that follows is mine. In no way could it be written chronologically, therefore I did not attempt it. The chapters are either obstacles that had to be overcome or a character that I needed to develop. It is the journey that I took to find harmony within all my being. I'm not a finished product, nor will I be. For many years, I wanted this life to end. I was tormented and unhappy, and blamed everyone for who I was. I am now fortunate to have a life worth living and am able to enjoy that life. Just as Christ paid a price for my healing, there was much I had to do to be able to receive it, hold onto it, and walk it out.

Introduction

I liken myself to the man described in Mark 5:5 — "And always night and day, he was in the mountains and in the tombs, crying out and cutting himself with stones." Always, never ceasing, no rest, no peace. Crying out! Not sitting still and holding it all in, but crying out. The scripture doesn't say that he was using words. He was in agony, tormented and at a loss for words. Howling like a dog chained outside that wants to be in the house with its owner. The mental anguish was too much to bear! Feeling physical pain helps dull the mental pain, so he cut himself with stones. He was wandering around the tombs. Each time I was wounded, I wanted to bury it and forget about it, but I wasn't always able. I'd hang out in the graveyard lamenting over all that had been done to me since the day I was born. Night and day, I was there, crying and dealing with mental anguish that no one will ever feel because it was caused by my wounds. No one can ever understand, as the memories were mine. No words can express the pain that caused me to howl. I didn't cut myself, but I did deliver self-beatings to the point of bruising. I stood at a mirror with a knife to my throat, yelling at the piece of garbage in the reflection: "Do it! Put the knife through your neck! Go for the jugular and bring an end to this thing called life." I was a tormented soul who wanted life to be finished with an irreversible ending. How does one go from this kind of existence to finding a life that is free from torment? In the pages to come, I want to bring you into my tormented being. Share with you the journey of a life that changed after meeting Jesus, who had compassion on me.

This book is dedicated to all who have struggled with being transgender and to those who have gone before me and may have regrets. No matter your actions, God still loves you. To those that are in the midst of the struggle: may you find the courage to seek out what God has for you.

There are many I could thank for helping me throughout my journey. My gratitude to Htoi Jones for grasping my vision for the cover, then creating it. Nichole for being one of the first to reach out to me, then never leave. I've been fortunate to sit under the leadership of two incredible pastors. Pastor Cleddie Keith, thank you for providing the environment for finding a deeper, meaningful relationship with God. Your wise council and encouragement will be with me forever. Pastor Jamey Bridges, thank you for taking me in after I was discarded. Both Pastors valued me, allowing me to learn to value myself. To Jane and Larry for being there at the beginning of my foundation building: your wise council guided me through many dark times. And lastly to Marylyn for the patience, guidance, and pulling me under your wing: you were a spiritual mother and so much more.

Most Important Day of My Life

I t was a late March Sunday in Kansas City. A blizzard had dumped snow across the Midwest. It was one of those pretty, wet snows that was lovely to look at but treacherous to drive in. I had spent the weekend with my fiancé as well as a group of friends. It was time to check out of the hotel and get ready to go our separate ways. First, we would take in a non-denominational church service. The routine of the last year had been to meet quarterly in a different place each time. Personally, I didn't care about the church service; it just extended my time with my friends.

I was hanging on to a relationship and giving it CPR in order for it not to die and wither away. My fiancée had moved back to Iowa a little over a year ago. We still saw each other monthly and talked on the phone almost every day. On the exterior, it was your normal long distance relationship. To know the details of how she ended up in Iowa and I was still in St. Louis, you would know it was anything but a normal relationship. This is why I went to the church service, why I drove over 600 miles monthly to be with her. To do life without her would take away my reason for living. I would do almost anything to keep us going, especially attending church.

Did I have something against church? No, but I didn't see the purpose in going. I was raised Catholic, in church every weekend and in CCD classes on Wednesday evenings. To be honest, I still don't know what CCD stands for. When I was young the classes were a chance to see my cousins. Sure, I memorized the prayers, was baptized as an infant, and met all the criteria to have my first communion. In all of that time, nobody reached my heart and gave me a reason to believe in something unseen. By my early teens, the youth group included my brother, which made me uncomfortable. Therefore, I never plugged into anything. At sixteen, I had a job and tried to make sure my schedule was during church services. Once I graduated and left home, I was no longer a churchgoer.

How does one go from being a self-acknowledged atheist to a church attendee? In my case, it was to keep my engagement alive. The day she announced she was moving back to Iowa was a day she had just left a church service. In my brilliant mind, I thought going to church would keep her beside me forever. After she left for Iowa, I found a church home in St. Louis. Going to church weekly made the quarterly Sunday services less painful. I actually enjoyed these Sundays over my home church. I had the option to get in my car and head for St. Louis, but I always made time to stay for an additional few hours.

This particular Sunday in KC was unlike any other. There was worship music. Mixed in with the music was a testimony by one of the band members. This particular band was a family. They had recently been involved in a horrible car accident in which their mother had died. They continued to share all the details surrounding the accident and tell us how difficult it was to lose their mother that way. Then they began speaking about the youngest girl. I was employed in the medical field. I spent my free time hanging out in the ER, helping wherever I could. During that time, I had picked up enough medical knowledge to know that the youngest sibling should have died in the accident, but that is not how their story ended. They spoke of the miracle healing she received. They attributed this miracle to God. A very loving God. My brain could not wrap itself around the fact that the person speaking was the person who should be dead, or at the very least in a vegetative state. My belief system was being challenged. It was going to take time to process all that they had shared. I didn't want to believe it, but she was standing onstage and talking. How could I deny it?

Next, they brought out the featured speaker, Stephanie Fast. It was the first time two testimonies were ever given in one service. My intellectual side had just been engaged. What was coming next would require my emotional side. It was the story of a child born in Korea to a Korean mother and an American GI. Biracial children were not accepted in Korea. At the age of four, Stephanie was abandoned by her mother and thrown out to provide for herself in a country where everyone hated her. Her story is full of tragedies that will rip out pieces of your heart. In my case, I learned that I actually had a heart that could be touched. Her story continued with being adopted by Americans as a teenager. She shared her struggles to allow herself to be loved and learn to love and trust Christ. In my mind, my life had been difficult. It was full of challenges that had left me with a hardened heart. This story made me question everything I had ever thought about my circumstances. To be unloved by your family is underwhelming compared to being despised by your entire country. Stephanie didn't have a place of refuge. I was fortunate enough to have a childhood friend's house that I could spend time at. Her mother often called me inside for one-on-one time. I didn't realize then how important her unconditional acceptance was until later in life. It was even longer before I understood just how important those moments were.

In the moments and hours that followed, my life changed forever. There was a call to the front for all who had been moved by the message. My girlfriend flew out of her seat, down several rows of stairs, and into the mass of people. I knew in that moment that our relationship as I knew it was over. No amount of CPR was going to keep it going. It was over, done, finished, terminated. She returned to our seats to say what I already knew. I left stunned, completely numb. If I had a thought, I couldn't tell you what it was. I just wanted to get in my car and head for St. Louis. I was so set on getting out of there that I completely ignored someone who tapped me on the shoulder. I never turned around, never stopped, and to this day have no idea who it was.

The roads were about halfway cleared. All of the bridges were covered with snow and ice. What should have been a four-hour trip to St. Louis became six hours. It was too much time for me to think. Definitely too much time to keep my emotions in check while stopping them from spinning out of control, followed by taking control. I couldn't think of any reason to live. Each time approached a bridge, I tried to figure out how I could spin off the road and kill myself. I had to be certain that it looked like an accident, and more importantly that I died. As I dwelled on the accidental death, I remembered that I have a cousin who lives about half way between Kansas City and St. Louis. I dropped in to see her, but she couldn't take away the pain of my breakup. None of my family, immediate or otherwise, were happy with the majority of my personal life choices. I had a reputation of being hardheaded and argumentative. At this time, my immediate family and I were not on speaking terms. This was completely my choice. I had blocked them out of my life as they continually didn't agree with my decisions. For example, when I was away to learn to be a radiology technologist, I had reached out to tell them I was not receiving the education they were paying for. After a trip to meet with the head instructor, their view was twisted so they believed that I was just a horrible student and person. They were told that I was spending my lunch breaks eating from the vending machine and then sleeping. I was shocked at how this upset them. For my last two years in high school, they didn't pay for me to eat a school lunch, nor did they provide any food from home that could be taken for lunch. I was confused as to why it was such a big deal now that I wasn't eating lunch. They completely believed him over anything I was saying to them. Once again, I was betrayed by those I should have been able to trust. Again, they proved how little they cared about me. It was disheartening. It was like I had been thrown in a well to crawl my way to the top, only to be stomped on so I would fall back to the bottom of the well. I believed I had to stay in that situation and tough it out. Hearing the speaker, Stephanie, made me realize that it was a good thing that they hadn't tossed me into the streets to fend for myself. They took responsibility for the life they had created by clothing me, paying for school, and providing shelter. All of this was good, but I wanted—no, I craved—to be loved. To be respected enough to have my opinion heard and validated. For a discussion to take place, then a decision made. Instead, they chose to believe lies that told them I was of little value.

I knew my cousin was a believer of Christ. My heart was being touched, and my mind was confused. I wanted to understand what had just happened and was still going on in me. I'm certain I caught my cousin off guard by showing up. I was looking for answers, although I am sure I never verbalized a question. I wanted her to read my mind and body language—to talk to me without me speaking and to understand without my sharing what was going on. I am not sure what I expected, but I left empty handed.

What was I going to do? As I said earlier, I had a home church. The church had a nice man named Mark contact me. Mark had been calling me often. He was trying to get me involved in a small group associated with the church. He was persistent with his calls, just as I was consistent in turning down all of his invitations. Upon leaving my cousin's house, I decided that I would get home, call Mark, and hope he could help me with the pain. As soon as I walked through the door, I called him. He was getting ready to go to the Sunday evening service and wanted me to meet him there. I was tired and needed to do laundry. He then invited me to meet him at his apartment later that evening. Interesting how I was too tired to go to church but had no problem meeting Mark at 10:30 at night. I would venture to say I was a little bit afraid of visiting a church again.

I headed to Mark's apartment, not sure what all I was going to share with him. In all honesty, I am not sure what I expected Mark to do for me. Mark was full of life and a joy to talk to. He had been trying to meet me in person and become more involved. I thought Sunday mornings were enough. I didn't want to make church my life. I was only trying to pump life into my engagement so that I could get married. I never went to a mid-week meeting. It stayed as a voice on the phone until I met Mark on this Sunday. Out of all the people I knew, it was Mark that I was calling. It doesn't make sense, nor will it ever. Then again, a new set of eyes on an old situation can always be of use.

I arrived at Mark's apartment complex. I sat in the car for several minutes, still trying to straighten out all of the thoughts that were swirling in my head. What could I say to him that would validate being at his home so late at night? I slowly headed inside and up the stairs, and knocked on his door. There he was smiling from ear to ear as he opened the door to welcome me into his home. We sat down across the living room from each other. He sensed how uncomfortable I was and started the conversation by asking me what was going on. I filled him in on the details of my life with my girlfriend and how it had ended that morning. We had been together approximately five years. I was unsure of where my life was headed now. Mark gave me that big grin and asked if I was ready to invite Jesus into my life. Now, Mark had been calling me for months. Every phone call ended with Mark asking me if I was ready to accept Christ. Each time I answered no, not tonight. This time, the question was asked face to face. This time I was hurting, lost, confused. I leaned back in the chair, and my life rolled through my head. I thought about all of the different vices I had in my life that I thought would bring me to a place of happiness. None had. Not one. Maybe for a moment, but not for very long. So many disappointments.

Mark sat patiently while I recounted my life. I finally made eye contact and said, "Why not?" Why not, what else was there left to try? I had no belief that this could make any difference in my life. Mark had been persistent. Meeting him for the first time gave me the ability to see that he was a happy dude. My life had been a rolling belief system. Catholic, atheist, and then calling myself agnostic. Now I was stepping into uncharted waters, not even sure of what I was agreeing to. Well, not really agreeing to, but going along with the idea of.

I didn't have a conviction of needing Jesus. I didn't understand what it meant to have Him in my life. I certainly did not understand the concept of a living God. I only knew I was at the end of my rope, with nowhere to turn. Mark didn't offer advice, He only offered a Savior. He didn't sugarcoat it or try to get me to understand my need. He made a statement: "You need this." My "why not" answer was all I could muster. I was a broken individual—broken in more ways than I could ever acknowledge at this moment. "Why not" was a statement instead of a question. There was no reason left not to. I certainly did not have any understanding of the Christian terminology of "getting saved," "yielding my life to Christ," and all the other Christianese mumbo jumbo. Mark had never veered from the words of saying I needed to invite Jesus into my life.

I followed Mark's lead in how to proceed with the invitation. To my surprise, I was overcome with joy. My "Why not" changed to "Why didn't I do this earlier?" I sat in this wonderful moment in time. I saw Mark's smile get even bigger. I didn't understand what was happening, but I knew I didn't care. It was in this moment that Jesus came off the pages of a book. He came into my life in a real way. Did I see Him? No. Did that make it any less real? Not at all. I didn't feel a need to see; I now believed.

My joy and peace were suddenly interrupted by the condemnation of who I was and what I was involved in. I was overwhelmed by the need to tell Mark everything that was going on. He could see the change in my demeanor. I fearfully looked at him and told him I needed to share more of my life. It was then that I dropped the bombshell that I was really a woman. You see, I had had my name changed and had been living under the identity of a male for almost two years. I was dressed like a male. By all appearances, I was a male.

The smile disappeared from Mark's face as he realized he was in his apartment alone with a female. Even though I felt how uncomfortable Mark was, he didn't immediately tell me to leave. He grabbed a Bible off of his bookshelf, handed it to me, and offered to pray for me. I so appreciate the fact that I never knew his opinion about what I was doing. The only advice he ever gave was that I should pray and ask God what I should do.

How awesome is that? In this day and age, when everyone has an opinion on everything, I was given the timeless advice to seek God and follow his direction. Mark could have thrown me out of his apartment and told me not even to return to the church, as my kind wasn't wanted. He didn't. He was unwavering in his belief that I needed Christ just as much in this moment as I would in the coming years.

Now What?

What I had believed was my future had suddenly become an unknown. How could I be so certain that this is what I needed to do to find peace within? Now I wasn't sure of anything in my life. Mark said I should pray. Did he not know that I had never prayed before? How do you pray? How do you hear from God and know what His direction is? So many questions and no answers. I was left with a book and the brief instructions to pray and ask God.

The next morning, I woke up, put on my dress shirt and tie, and then left for work. I was always depressed and moody. Would my coworkers notice anything different about me? Well, why would they? I enjoyed my work life, the people, the environment, and even my boss, Sue. I did have that one coworker who was outspoken about his religion. I sought him out and told him about my weekend. I asked him where I should begin reading my Bible. I got a blank stare and a few mumbled words: anywhere I wanted to. Geez, wasn't he helpful. There are people who think the outside should change equally with the inside. I hadn't changed outwardly, so in his mind, how could I have changed inwardly? He couldn't meet my question with any answers, as he was still too busy judging my appearance.

Maybe God had a plan. Could it be that He was jealous enough that he didn't want me seeking anyone else's advice? In retrospect, I now know that is exactly what was happening. God wanted me to learn to lean on Him, to seek Him for guidance. Proverbs 3: 5–6 (NLT)

Trust in Lord with all your heart,
Do not depend on your own understanding;
Seek His will in all you do,
And He will show you which path to take

My experiences had taught me not to trust, as I had been hurt by those closest to me, those I should have been able to have had safekeeping with. Yet, I had gone from unbelief in God to unwavering trust in a matter of seconds. I wanted to know His way for me to go. I just didn't understand how to get that answer. I love the analogy of talking to an empty chair. Put the Lord in that chair and start talking. He is unseen, yet always present, in good times and bad. I wasn't talking to an empty chair yet, but I was certainly mumbling under my breath a lot. I was trying to hang on to the life I had made at the same time as trying to figure out what God had for me. Wrestling, yet not realizing that this was what I was doing. It was a good thing, but all the same, I didn't enjoy where I was.

I wanted to hear God before I made any other moves in my life. I had been cross-dressing and living under a male identity for almost two years. It was my intent to have my biological body equal the name and gender on my driver's license. I had been planning this for almost five years, trying to save the money to do so. I was doing everything that was in the guidebook on how to prepare for gender reassignment surgery. After all of this time, how could I be stuck not understanding my future?

I was in a room alone, doing paperwork. Mindless paperwork, a job everyone in my department hated. It was late on this Wednesday afternoon, the Wednesday after I accepted Christ. With a pure heart, I spoke this question to the Lord: "Do you want me to go back to being the woman I was born as?" This was a very real, pure question. In my mind, I had been born the wrong sex. I was only aiming to fix what seemed so wrong in my life. In that moment, I heard God's audible voice. I never heard an audible voice since. I was at a critical juncture in my life. It was so early in my Christian journey that I had not learned to hear the voice of my Shepherd. It was such a power-filled moment that I almost fell off my chair. Maybe I did start to fall off, as I immediately stood and went to my boss's office.

Sue was working away as I walked in and closed the door behind me. Her office was situated in the middle of our suite, having two doors to enter. As I closed the one behind me she turned to close the other. Sue knew that I was cross-dressing, so what I had to say was fairly easy. I informed her that I was giving my notice to resign. She was a little shocked by my statement, asking if I had a problem within the office. My answer was simple: I needed to stop cross-dressing. It would be easiest to quit and find new employment. God doesn't ask us to walk the easiest way. He asks us to put our trust in Him and walk the path that is laid out before us. According to my plan, I would resign, get my name changed back, start dressing as a female, let my hair grow, and find a new place of employment. God's plan was that I should keep my job and move forward with regaining the identity that He gave me upon birth. Having an income proved to be the better way.

Sue was willing to go to the board and explain what was happening. I was a good worker, and she wanted me to stay with the company. How could I walk away from that? She asked me to meet individually with my coworkers to explain the change. This is the reason I wanted to leave. I wanted to save face, hide my pre-Christian life, not explain my new choices, and just get on with my life. Instead I painfully met with each individual I worked with. I was met with hatred for many different reasons. To this day, I cannot comprehend why some people felt that they needed to share their opinion. Some were all for me being a woman. Others spoke of what a great man I made and that I should press forward with what I had been trying to accomplish. I even had one woman who was extremely upset that the name I had been using was her brother's. I assure you that when I chose my name, I didn't know this woman or her brother. I laugh about it today, as hindsight is 20/20.

At the time, each of the comments took a chunk of me, driving me into a life of isolation. To share openly and in return receive hostile remarks was disheartening, and it sucked. Nobody would ever understand how difficult life had been. For so long I had felt like I was trapped in the wrong skin. A man held captive in a woman's body. I had been doing what I believed would lead me to a place of peace and happiness. I had fought the good fight. Gone to the extremes of seeking gender reassignment surgery. Now, I had been given an opportunity to find a way to the place of peace and happiness. I was grappling for what that way was. Inside, I knew this was right. I should not trust my feelings and thoughts, but to grab hold of what I believed God was guiding me to do. Having to explain my decisions was not on my agenda. However, this was the position I was in. Each discussion felt like a debate. The point of meeting was to advise my coworkers about what I was going to do. Instead, I found myself in the place of feeling the need to explain my actions. Not only explain, but back it up with some logic. I didn't have statistics to hand people. I didn't have anyone else I knew who I could use as an example. This was my choice. My choice alone. Their opinions were not sought out, but were spoken. My choice was analyzed, discussed, debated, hated, and possibly accepted. Each meeting drained me to exhaustion. I'm certain you will not be surprised to hear that the comments did not end here. It would be accurate to say that I was the topic around the water cooler for all the years that followed while I was working for Sue. To be robbed of an opportunity to meet someone before they could have a tainted opinion was disheartening. I came to the point of never trying to get to know the new person. I waited to see if they would approach me. My expectation was rejection. I began to accept the isolation as my depression grew deeper.

Human nature is hard to predict, but I think it is accurate to say that once you are a source of gossip, you will stay a hot topic. It's fair to say that any new coworker was brought up to speed on my past before a week went by. The most frustrating part of that is that no one talked to me to gain an understanding of what I was doing. The facts of why I did what I did were not necessary. Only the gossipers' opinions of my actions were pertinent to their conversation. Life became overwhelming. The confusion increased. It all led to me questioning my choices. I was more alone than I had ever been in my life. I was frustrated that I had ever sought out gender reassignment surgery. For so many years, I had known I was different. There was something about me that just didn't fit in. When I realized that I was being held captive in a woman's body, it brought some relief to know what was wrong. With it came a whole new set of circumstances that meant acceptance of where I was at. Going forward to seek the surgery only came after I had fallen in love with Grace. I wanted to have her beside me with a way to have what I saw as a normal life and to be a part of a family. Now I was even angry that I had ever met Grace. That I had even sought out the surgery. I was angry about everything.

I didn't enjoy my work environment any longer. Each day it was harder to get out of bed for work, for church, even for pleasure. Nothing was fun anymore. It was still early in my Christian journey, and I was now wavering in my beliefs. Every moment of my life seemed to be an event that caused a storm. I could not keep withstanding the storms. Everything I touched became a disaster. I couldn't risk any more failures, so I quit trying. I quit living and went into survival mode. I was only doing what was necessary for that day. I eventually felt that the only safe place to be was in bed, asleep. Sleep was the only way to get through the days. I was only awake long enough to work. I was slowly withering away, and questioning everything.

I couldn't doubt that I heard God's audible voice. I knew this was what God wanted me to do. Every step in a Godly direction was difficult. The only thing I knew to do for myself was to change my name back, update my wardrobe, and let my hair grow. They were all external changes, and each one presented different challenges. It was a snap to change my name from female to male. New driver's license, social security card, insurance, and utilities. To change back? Ha! Matthew 7:14: "Because narrow is the gate and difficult is the way which leads to life, and there are few who find it." I wanted to give in and not worry about the final few utility companies. The phone company would not, absolutely would not change the name without speaking to the male me at the same time as the female me. I got the help of a male friend to finally get the task completed. The gas company? I bet that customer service rep is still reeling from my call. This was the final one. My patience was gone, and she took the brunt of it. I pleaded with her to change the name. She was standing firm that she couldn't. She needed something more to change the name. I finally shouted at her, "Haven't you ever heard of a sex change?" With that, the name was changed in an instant.

I'm not proud of that moment. I'm only trying to point out how tedious it was to undo everything I had worked so hard to create. I had given away my God-given identity. To regain that identity was a battle. I even had an encounter with the law during this time. I hadn't changed my driver's license back yet, and then forgot it at my desk. I went out to do an errand over lunch and promptly was pulled over. I was standing on the side of the road with the officer, trying to explain that he would not find the female me in the system. He would have to run my male name. While I was cross-dressing, I had been told that if I was arrested, I should call an attorney as quickly as possible. A police officer had the option to put me in with whatever population he felt like. Either place would surely bring a beating from fellow inmates. This particular officer was a gentleman. He even made a joke about my trying to get out of a ticket, as no one had ever tried this one on him before.

I appreciated his professional handling of the matter and gladly paid my fine.

To be advised by an attorney that he should be my first call in the event of arrest shows the lengths I was willing to go to. Changing one's gender is not easy, either. There will always be haters in the world. Hate is one thing; it is a whole new level when it comes to violence. Disagree with me, yell at me, OK. Beat me up and possibly kill me, all because you don't agree with what I am doing? How does that solve anything? Obviously, the attacker is not looking for an agreeable solution. It still was a fear that I had to live with daily. Would violence become real in my life because of the clothes I was wearing? Now I was walking the opposite way, only to meet an entire new opposition. Life had become strenuous. I wanted out. I love the way a friend spoke of the moment she thought about taking her own life. It wasn't that she wanted to die, but that she no longer wanted to be in the circumstances that surrounded her. She wanted out.

I had worked in the medical field long enough to know that if you botched your suicide attempt, you could very well end up a vegetable, trapped in a body that no longer was functional. Still intact with any lingering pain and a mind that might never be able to form words. I had a healthy respect for making sure that if I was going to do it, it needed to be done adequately. I turned into a suicide planner, which became a coping mechanism. Every day I thought about how I could kill myself. What day would be the best? How awful it would be if I messed up somebody else's day. I'd pick a cold winter day to jump into a river. Or maybe I could get the right combination of drugs to take. I believed that God wanted me, but did not see anything that proved that this was accurate. I wanted to believe there was something better than what I was experiencing now. It wasn't the case. If I invited Christ into my life, it was all supposed to be better! Why wasn't it? Was the defect in me too great to be overcome? Was God having buyer's regret? Too many questions, too much doubt. Faith was diminishing as the sadness grew, and I spent more time sleeping.

I realize now that my expectations were inaccurate. As a new believer, I was led to believe in the beautiful, peaceful garden that awaited me. A place where I would walk with God and He would love me, and protect me from all harm, and I would live happily ever after. Where did that dream-filled expectation come from? Straight from the churched people. It certainly didn't do me any favors by giving me false hopes. **The reality is that the circumstances you are in will not change the moment you click your heels together as you invite Christ into your life. The truth is that you gain an incredible companion who will not leave your side, no matter how ugly it gets.** One who wants only good for you in a world that is full of horrible tragedies. The journey together begins. You aren't given a pass to start over. Troubles don't just disappear. The major difference is not having to be alone in making decisions. Choices aren't easier; in fact, they may be much harder! I had been on my own, believing I knew what was best. Seeking another opinion and learning to trust it really was a better way, but it was unquestionably difficult. As with most choices, you don't see the result right away. As I slowly saw that following God's lead would give me a better life, my trust in Him and His ways grew. For me, it certainly didn't happen on day one, or even in year one.

The day finally arrived: the rubber band that was holding me together snapped. I arrived at work on a Monday morning, looked at my coworker, and advised her that I was going back home. I no longer had what it took to get through a day in me. I made a call to my ex, Grace, leaving a message on her answering machine stating that somebody needed to help me. I knew I was in desperate need of intervention. I did not know where to turn, what to do. By the time I returned home, Grace had left a message for me. She advised me that I needed to call the Suicide Hotline. She was an eight-hour drive away. She couldn't help. It would be best to talk to someone trained to meet me where I was at. She requested that I call her back after I completed my call. I called the hotline, only to be met with a busy signal. I guess I wasn't the only one having a difficult Monday morning. I waited a few minutes and called again, busy, call, busy, call, and still busy. This was too much for me, so I did what I do best: I went to sleep.

I left the phone off the hook, not really thinking about the consequences of that decision. I just wanted to sleep uninterrupted. Escape from the reality that was going on around me. I awoke several hours later. I felt refreshed and ready to take on the world again. I called into work to talk to Sue. She was not available, but my call was transferred to a coworker who kept me on the phone until she was. I am so thankful that I stayed working for her. She cared about me as a person more than I could believe. She had seen this day coming and already had an appointment scheduled for me with a psychiatrist. Then she informed me that I was not allowed to come back to work until the doctor released me to. Wow, what was I going to do until Wednesday afternoon? I had the option of going to an ER, but I couldn't figure out what I would say as to why I was there. Did I need an ER? I was blind to the condition I was in mentally and too embarrassed to admit it to anyone else. I tried to call Grace back and ended up with her machine. Honestly, I was upset that she wasn't there to take my call so many hours later. I called a mutual friend who talked to me for a few minutes and then asked to speak to Grace. I was completely confused; why would he ask to talk to Grace? In my hesitation, he asked if she had arrived yet. I was stunned to find out that she was on her way to my home. When she arrived, I completely collapsed on the floor. All I had left in tank was gone, and now I didn't have to think or make any decisions. Someone I loved was there to look after me. I sat on the floor and cried. I was unable to answer any of Grace's questions—even the simple one of what should we do for dinner. Life had overwhelmed me. She stayed with me through the appointment time. To my surprise, I was directly admitted to the psych ward. Grace went to my home, packed a suitcase, returned to the hospital, and then went back to Iowa. Once in Iowa, she called my parents to tell them where I was. I hadn't talked to them to tell them of the breakup. I still didn't see any reason to communicate with them. I was surprised when I got their phone call of concern.

Most Important Day Of My Life

I spent a week as an inpatient and an additional week as an outpatient. Then I was released to return to work. I had been gone long enough that if the rumor mill had settled at all, it was now stirred back up again. Sue was amazing in so many ways; what came next was more than I could have ever expected. She asked that I bring her every medical bill that came my way. My company was going to pay the bills with an interest-free loan. What? Seriously? They didn't want me to have additional stress worrying about the bills. At this time, I was too young to see the favor God had given me with my employer. His hand was on me even as I was drifting away from Him.

I spent the next few months wandering. Maybe wondering would be a better word to use. Wondering about every decision I had made in life. Wondering why I hadn't killed myself on my twenty-fifth birthday like I vowed to do in high school. I was still going to church, but I was also beginning to wonder why. I spent most of my evenings with a friend who was battling cancer. I either went to her home to play cards or picked up tacos to take to her in the hospital. She was a co-worker who was out on medical leave, and her son had been my attorney. I cared a great deal about her, and when she lost her battle, I lost a huge piece of myself. I had taken her to church, had her prayed over for healing. That prayer was not answered — at least not in the way I wanted it to be. Now my evenings were empty, and my days were filled with whispering. My inner turmoil was building, and my outward signs of struggle were apparent. The doctors gave me additional happy pills, but I was more interested in seeing the bottom of a bottle. Antidepressants and alcohol do not go together, so I gave up the happy pills. I looked human, talked like one and walked like one, but I was hollow inside. I was functioning on autopilot, in survival mode. This was a mechanism that would carry me through the next two decades of my life.

I took on an evening part-time job. This was a productive way to fill my evenings. It helped me pay back my debt and eventually became my new full-time employment. Leaving Sue was a difficult decision, but it was wonderful to get away from being the subject of office gossip. To have a clean slate and move forward with life. Unfortunately, I didn't know how to move forward. It was really just a change in scenery. I was no longer going to church, was no longer in a relationship. My life didn't have a foreseeable future, and I was still angry about everything.

Processing What Just Happened

First, let us break down the Christianese mumbo jumbo. At this point in time, I was coming from the place of not believing that Jesus was anything more than a character in a story. To believe in a character would be like the person who gets so wrapped up in a TV show that they cry over what happens to that character. The storyline isn't real events causing emotion within the audience. If there was a God with a Son named Jesus, then why had my life been one painful event after another? I didn't need a TV show to cry over; my life events could do that for me. Instead of having emotions, I found many ways to avoid thinking about them, feeling them, and dealing with them. I dwelled on suicidal thoughts to end this reality of who I was. To be saved would mean that one needed help. I didn't need to be "saved." I had only felt disappointments throughout my life. There wasn't anyone I was ever going to trust to get close to me. My belief was that anyone who stated they loved me was ultimately going to leave me in the most painful way possible. I believe that Grace and I ended up together because I needed rescued, and she needed to be a rescuer. Because of my experience with her, I was adamant that I was not going to put myself in the position of needing another person again.

Yielding my life to Christ, or giving my life over to Him. Seriously? I don't even believe He is more real than what I am watching on television. How can I yield to something I do not see, much less do not believe is even real? To have faith in something, someone, that I didn't believe existed was the challenge. Nobody ever even tried. I was written off by all who knew me. I only knew insults. I feared being told I was loved. I had a boundary line that I defended. To keep peace with me and be my friend was a high-maintenance job. If you succeeded, I was a friend, advocate, and defender in return. If you did not succeed, I had no time for you, and if you continued to try to gain access, I was at war with you. It shouldn't be a surprise that I was not approached with the proposition of believing in Christ.

That leaves me in the position of trying to explain how to understand the process of going from an unbeliever to a believer. It is so hard to explain that I think these Christianese words were thrown out there as an attempt to capture the process in one word. In my story, the church acquaintance, Mark, presented me with the assurance: "You need to do this." I had exhausted every avenue to find peace on my own. Why not try this? Simply put, it was extending an invitation to Jesus. Say what? My home was my personal space. If you came to my door uninvited, I wouldn't greet you. I left you at the door knocking, wondering if I was there or not. Did I not want people in my home? Yes. I only wanted them there on my terms. It is the same with my personal space. I didn't want anyone within my space bubble; it caused me to be ugly if you came into my space uninvited. Let's imagine standing at the door to your home, your personal space. You know that someone is on the other side. They haven't knocked, nor done anything to require you to respond to their presence. You have a choice, your personal choice. It is not a choice another can make for you. Do you extend the invitation? Or do you walk away from the door and never open it? It is the same decision that awaits an unbeliever. Do I open my life up to make room for Jesus? Or do I never open it to see what it is all about?

I had many wounds and disappointments, and a complete lack of trust in humanity. The only thing that remained for me to try that might possibly have a positive impact on my life was to open that door. Not just a crack to see who it is, but to open it and extend an invitation to come in. The invitation is the first step. I decided to invite Jesus to be in my life and in my personal space — to yield to His will over mine. I decided to have faith in something that I didn't believe was real. Faith means to trust and believe. I decided to relinquish my trust in myself and to put trust in Him. Obviously, I wasn't getting myself anywhere close to a life that was meaningful or peaceful. Inviting Jesus to be a part of my life and yielding to Him was a process that required a lot from me.

I will never regret extending that invitation. Relinquishing control is a whole other process that cannot be explained in one sentence. Nor does it happen at the same time as the invitation is extended. It is only the beginning. Moving beyond extending the invitation requires only knowing that the One you are entrusting yourself to has your best interests in mind. **Asking someone who doesn't trust to allow anything to lead is a scary proposition. Moving forward requires keeping that trust that you had the moment you extended the invitation.** Thus, you begin your personal journey as a believer, a follower. It is a personal journey, even though you are sharing it with others. You cannot follow in another's footsteps, as these may not be the ones God has ordained for you. Human nature is to compare ourselves to others. To imitate successful people. However, God has created you to be you. He desires a personal relationship with you. Don't follow others; follow the only One who wants to lead you to a life that is worth living. The man that I compared myself to from Mark 5:5 was crazed by the pain he was in. Screaming and tormented, a life of turmoil. At the end of the story, you will find that after his encounter with Jesus, he was found sitting with Jesus, clothed and in his right mind. He had found peace, a life that could be lived free from torment. I wanted nothing less than this.

Hopefully you have offered a place for Jesus in your personal space. Where do we go from here? Well, to church would be an obvious answer. However, I am urging you to find a personal relationship with your Heavenly Father. As with building any relationship, you must get to know one another. Reading the Bible is a way to begin to understand the nature of God. God is love of the purest form. Many have received love, but it is a fallible, human love. God's love will never leave. Does that mean he will not discipline us? No. It means that in His unfailing love, He will guide us and discipline us in a perfect, loving way. He never leaves nor forsakes us. That is something that my human mind could not understand. Everyone left me as soon as the road became bumpy. Not my Heavenly Father. He has stood by through all of my messes and all the mistakes I made in my zeal to share about Him. Even when I fell and had my faith shaken and walked away from Him, He stayed constant, never moved or upset by my behavior. He was always waiting for me to return to Him and find His merciful love once again.

Learn to talk to God. Yeah, I get it. Talking to something you can't see is crazy. I have found that it is crazy not to. Verbalizing what is in my head as God already knows my thoughts and the circumstances of what is happening in my life. Asking for his guidance and learning to hear His responses. How many times have you tried to talk to someone about what is happening only to be interrupted by their opinions and thoughts on the matter? I personally find that extremely frustrating, as I usually just need to get it out so that I can move on from that moment. So, what is wrong with talking to your loving Father, who will listen until you are exhausted from talking? At that moment, you sit in the stillness, in the quiet, and wait. Yes, wait. In the world of instant gratification, learning to wait is difficult. Wait. Psalm 62:5 (NLT): "Let all that I am wait quietly before God, for my hope is in Him." Continuing to verse 8, "O my people, trust in Him at all times. Pour out your heart to Him, for God is our refuge." Man will disappoint you. God will not. You may *feel* like He has, but He has not. His ways are not ours. Nor can we comprehend what He may be trying to accomplish.[2]

Sitting alone with God has proven to be some of the sweetest moments of my life. Learning to trust and obey is difficult. But as God has been faithful, trusting has come quicker. I still have doubts, questions, and concerns. God has continued to be the same. Why He loves me? I really don't understand why. Accepting His love was years in the making. I don't like to admit that this was one of the hardest parts of becoming a believer. I certainly don't like telling you that it didn't happen within the first five years of my walk with Him. When I began to really believe and accept it, I'm really not sure. I believe I can admit that it was over ten years. Again, I'm being transparent. I was not transformed overnight. I fought with God even though I believed in Him and knew He had my best interests in mind. Did I mention that God is patient?

My hope in sharing my story is to help you understand how to get a fulfilling life with God much more quickly than I did. Learn from my hard-headedness. Understand that there is hope when it appears all is lost.

Control

I want to define control as the power to influence or direct people's behavior or the course of events. I've got the power. No, I *needed* to have the power. Throughout my life there had been hurt, abuse, and feelings that I had been tossed out with the garbage more than once. None of that was going to happen again if I could help it. There was a huge step in learning to be with God. It was a leap to learn to lay down my desires and thoughts. Just to begin yielding to God's plan and purpose and adopting His thoughts. Laying down control? Oh, I said it! If you have never met a control freak, I am happy for you. I don't know anyone who doesn't like being in control. Some do have the gift of not needing to be the one in charge. Being in control of what happens to me personally was an issue I had, but I never realized how deeply it ran. If you would have asked me if I was a control freak, I would have answered no. I enjoyed driving, so I always offered to drive. I had no realization that it was a need for me to be the driver. When I was driving, it was up to me how we got to our destination, or even if we made it. How fast or slow we got there. If you rode with me, you know it was always fast. Did I mention that I didn't have patience?

My need to be in control was not overtly obvious to me. Others could see it. In certain circumstances, my need to control was greater than that of others. Understanding to the point of accepting was not something that happened quickly, nor was it painless. Why did I need to be in control? I wanted to put limitations on others in order to be in charge of their actions. Pain caused by others was what drove me. I didn't want to be disappointed by another person. Trust had to be earned; it was not granted with an introduction. I don't remember a time when I trusted anyone. I can't think of a time when I *felt* that another had my best interests at heart, or that they wouldn't leave when something better came along.

As a child, I had a terrible fear of thunderstorms. My perception was that every storm would be accompanied by a tornado. This fear grew into the feeling that any rain with wind was dangerous. Then, as I was taught which clouds might produce tornados, the lines became blurred, and I was unsure which clouds could produce a tornado and which were just ones that filled the sky without harm. I didn't cry or act hysterically; I just always had my eye on the sky, awaiting the tornado. My childhood home didn't have a basement. In order for us to have appropriate shelter, we had to get to the neighbor's house and into their basement. To assure that we always had access to their home, we had a key that my parents kept on top of the tall china cabinet in the dining room. As a child, I could not reach the key, even if I stood on a chair. It was completely out of my reach. When the perceived storms would come during the night, my solution was to sleep in my parents' room. I didn't dare wake them, as I knew they wouldn't have any understanding of or patience with my fear. Instead, I slept on the floor next to the bed. The goal was to be where I would be tripped over if my dad arose to take the family next door. My thought wasn't that when he tripped over me, he would get me to safety. It was so that he would wake me up, and I could make sure that I got myself there. I had no trust that they wouldn't leave me behind. This behavior frustrated my dad immensely. When he would wake in the morning, with no indication of the storm that had passed during the night, he had no warning that I was going to be on the floor to trip him. I don't recall any open conversation about my behavior in which my parents could gain an understanding of why I did the things I did. Even if there had been one, I am not sure that I could have verbalized or explained my actions. He wanted me to stop sleeping on the floor, and I refused. I was not going to give up my sense of safety, one of my few forms of self-protection. Whatever punishment was given was fine by me, as I was not going to change. I didn't until I was tall enough to reach the key for myself.

This was the way I stayed. I learned that being defiant of my parents' wishes was ok. All of their punishments didn't faze me. It actually became an expectation. If they verbalized their frustrations or told me how they wanted me to act, my heart would immediately harden. My inner thought was "That will never happen." It was no longer about what was best for me. It was all about staying in control. I cannot explain why I needed control at this young age; I can only tell you that their wants meant nothing to me. I was a child making childish decisions, believing I could only rely on myself to meet my needs. As I got older and older, the hindrances of this childish thinking were a major stumbling block. Problem solving was not a skill I took with me into adulthood. What did go with me was a lack of respect for any authority figure. My inability to express myself in words led to an inability to resolve conflicts. I lost many friendships over my inability to let go of control, to find common ground. My solution was to walk away and start over. I left many behind in disbelief, completely unaware of anything that they did. In all honesty, they didn't do anything. I would rather start over whenever I perceived conflict or felt they were getting to close. If I allowed you to become close, then you would see who I really was. Seeing me for who I was meant that you wouldn't like what you would see, causing you to leave. The separation had to be on my terms. That was my being in control. I didn't care about the path of destruction I left behind, nor did I care that I caused you any pain. Your feelings were not my concern. Just as a tornado destroys towns as a force of nature, I am certain that I left a wake of destruction behind me.

The first step to changing any behavior is recognition and acceptance of the truth of how it affects life. Accepting the need for change is one of the most difficult facts of life. After all, I have spent an entire life being a control freak who was willing to walk away from anything I couldn't control. It was all I knew. How could change happen? The willingness to start having permanent relationships required growing pains. I needed to learn how to be open as well as honest while accepting correction, and most importantly that long-term friends were more important than being right. I needed to gain the understanding that my perception wasn't always accurate. Misunderstandings are part of life. I needed to humble myself to admit I didn't have understanding, and ask questions until I could see the facts for what they really were. As I took on this improbable task of letting go of control, I found myself in uncomfortable positions too many times. This is my way of saying I was a slow learner. Fortunately, I was blessed to be with women in my church who were patient and kind, and they were able to call me out on my behaviors while challenging me to change. Listening to them speak truth to me was never easy. Understanding that God was using them to shape my life wasn't even a thought in my mind, but that is exactly what was happening. **God loved me so much that He put people in my life who wouldn't leave no matter how hard I pushed them to go.** They would love me no matter how ugly I got with them. I would yell at them, hang up on them, and shut the door, all to have them come right back to hold my hand while God was shaping me. Folks, let's be honest — these women were true disciples of Christ. They asked for nothing in return from me, knowing that their reward would come from God alone.

It is also important to note that it wasn't just one person trying to help me grow and change. I would have worn one person out. They banded together to rotate through. Each one had a different approach, or a gift, if you will. Their boundaries were as firm as their acceptance of me for who I was. Each of these women will always be with me. I may not see them any longer, but they left pieces of themselves with me. Their voices go through my head as I continue in my attempt to be a better me. They imparted priceless wisdom that I may not have allowed them to know I was listening to. All the same, it has stuck with me. It was up to me to take it or to ignore it. Isn't that what life is: choice after choice?

When did I let go of control completely? I'm not sure I have yet. I still like to drive. It is my goal to seek God in all I do. My human nature is still here, and I certainly have times when I believe I know best. I eventually exhaust my ways and find myself back at His feet, resting and waiting for guidance as to what I should do next.

Yielding

I n order to let go of control, I had to learn how to yield my thoughts and ways. I think yield is a word that can be misused or not completely understood. I used to live in the suburbs, and the drive to work was an adventure every day. I often felt like I was either in a race or was playing dodge the trucks. I never considered owning a small vehicle, as I knew that it increased my chances of being run off the road or completely destroyed in an accident with a more powerful, larger vehicle. To yield on the road means that the driver must slow down as they are approaching the intersection. They must be prepared to stop and yield the right of way to vehicles in and approaching the intersection. You must come to a full stop at a yield sign if traffic conditions require it. I have been told by another that on the interstate, the cars that are already there need to make room for the ones that are attempting to merge. Hmm, I don't think that's how it is written in the law. Honestly, how many have that thought? "Everyone needs to make room for me. Ready or not, here I come!"

In my years of rush hour driving, I have seen several different types of drivers. Each one is a great way to look at the various degrees of yielding. First, you have the polite driver. This is one who turns the blinker on to indicate the desire to change lanes. They patiently wait until another makes room for them. The opposite of that is the driver who begins their lane change while turning on the blinker. They are coming into your lane whether you like it or not. These are on opposite sides of the spectrum, with several scenarios that I could list in between. The worst driver is the one who comes into your lane with no prior indication of intended movement, and space for them is not of any concern to them. This was my perception of God. He not only wanted in my lane, but in my car.

For my purpose, I would like to define *yield* as to give way to submit, give consent, or grant permission. Finally, to allow. This is what I had to learn: to allow God to work in my life. As I approached intersections in my life, I slowly had to learn to sit and wait for God to lead. My usual way would be to blow through with whatever seemed right. I may ask an opinion from another, but it wasn't likely that I was going to listen to any advice. I had learned to do whatever I felt was right. You may have noticed that I have emphasized *feel* in previous pages. It is easy to go about life letting feelings lead the way. If it feels right, do it. If I felt like going out to drink the night away, then I did it. If I felt like not going to work, I would call in sick. If I felt like I was being treated unfairly at my job, I found another. I fully believe in the saying that my perception is my reality. The truth of any given situation didn't matter. Whatever I perceived to be truth would determine my actions. This is being led by feelings. As an adult, being led by feelings can cause issues. Stopping to discern truth may be the harder way to go. This ultimately was what I had to do. I couldn't be led by feelings and perception. They would fail me time and time again. Slowing down to find out what God had for me was not an easy process. Yielding to the point of surrender would be the goal. Is that an attainable goal? For me it was one of the most difficult places to attempt to be. I didn't trust. I had been hurt multiple times. Why would I want to yield to what God wanted? Wasn't He just going to set me up for more heartache? I couldn't just grant Him trust and control of my life. After all, it was my life.

It is my life. I can choose to do with it what I want. Do you see me sticking my tongue out at you? I can be a spoiled brat. I can throw a temper tantrum with the best, as I want my way and I want it now. If this is what I want to do, then I dare you to say something against it. Isn't it interesting that God gave us all free will to do just that? Whatever we want whenever it pleases us. Then when things go wrong, we shake our fists at Him and yell about why something happened. I know I did this. Sometime into my journey with Him, I moved to another city to help in an inner city ministry. I was excited about going. It was a wonderful experience. Three years after I moved, the ministry closed. Watching it die to the point of closure was distressing. I shook my fist at God. Why would you have me move here? I left the town where my brother was. He had two children in those years. I could have been the in-town aunt for them. I was certainly focused on me and my desires with this anger. Once my anger subsided, with the passing of time, I have been able to see what God did in my life during those years. The people I met and the experiences I had were all invaluable. Understanding God's ways should come with a manual. Oh wait, there is one. It is called the Bible. I can hear people moaning now saying, "I don't understand what I am reading." I think that could be exactly the point. I have conversations with people where I don't think I am understanding the point they are trying to make. I keep asking questions for clarification until I have the ah-ha moment. To form a relationship with God requires reading His word and having a conversation about it. To gain understanding, to find wisdom, and to begin to trust. All of this made surrendering my will to His easier. Did I like every path God led me down? Not really. It required faith to believe that He had my back and that His purpose would lead to good. It took even greater trust to accept that I may never understand the way I was guided or see the intended result.

In the early days of my journey, I was pure and genuine in my desire to find God's will and yield to it. God made His will known in that I should stop cross-dressing and return to the life of a female. To yield to God on this seemed simple, and a relatively clear process. I took this and tried to run with it. I didn't stop again to ask how I should proceed. It was a painful lesson that led to my walking away from God. Did He change His mind? No. Did I go the direction He wanted? Yes. However, when heading to any destination, there are several paths that will take you somewhere different from where you started. My hometown is in Iowa. I love Iowa and its square miles. Often, when driving through the state, I would take back roads while rarely looking at a map. This thought makes me laugh about what I would have done to the GPS lady. Recalculating until she blew a fuse. I knew that for every left turn, I would need to make a right turn. First going west, then heading north. Each time, I would end up at my intended destination and enjoy a different view. Once I knew God's will, I took off on the trip with a roadmap in my mind that was the fastest way from point A to point B. It's funny—God never told me to complete the process in a week. I never stopped between steps to see how I should proceed from there. I stopped asking, and He stopped guiding. The communication breakdown began. My yielding ended, and my anger grew. I turned off the guidance system.

This rest stop on my journey would last almost two years. Calling it a rest stop is almost hysterical. I did everything but rest. I accused God of playing a dirty trick on me by pretending to accept me for who I was and then laughing and saying, "Just kidding." The truth was, I stopped seeking. I stopped asking. I stopped all form of communication. I was filled with hate, as this perceived rejection was painful.

Anger

The saying is, "misery loves company." I am living proof of the accuracy of that statement. Misery could be defined as a state or feeling of great distress or discomfort of mind or body. *Discomfort of mind*, isn't that a sweet way to say *mean*? How about *wretched*? My personal favorite is *tormented*: severe mental anguish. How about the saying, "When mama ain't happy, nobody's happy"? So much truth to both sayings. I wasn't one who ran around complaining about my woes to others. I was the one who made sure if I was in a bad mood, you were going to be in one, too. I couldn't stand to be around contented people. I hated you for no reason other than that you appeared to be happy. I wanted to wipe that smile off your face at all costs. I was a pro at it, too. I was sneaky and would seize any opportunity I saw. One of my worst offences was to take a coworker's keys. In my arrogant opinion, she had life easy: a great mother, who I also worked with, and an incredible relationship with her entire family. She was always dropping her car keys anywhere in the office. The day came when the keys and I were alone in a room. I picked them up, put them in my pocket, and stayed silent as we all looked for them. I share this story to be transparent. If I didn't like you, I was a mean son of a gun. If I liked you or felt you had a tough life, then I was your best friend. I bent over backwards to do whatever I could to help you in any way. Normally it was either extreme, but I could be unmoved by you as well. I can't explain my behavior. At the time, I wasn't upset by it greatly. Today I remember those times and use them to fuel my desire to be a better fellow human being.

To say I had an anger issue would probably be an understatement. I hid my pain well, with quick wit and a decent sense of humor. However, I could change in less than a second. I often summed up my feelings about my anger with the statement, "I am not the person you want to meet in a dark alley, as I would beat you up just for the heck of it." I was keenly aware that if I was in a physical fight, I would kill, as I knew that once I started throwing punches, I would not be able to stop. The rage built up inside would take over, coming out in each blow delivered. I also knew that I couldn't handle time in prison, so the saying, "If you can't do the time, don't do the crime" was often a motto I lived by. This motto kept me from ever throwing a punch, but also led to a near-constant state of anxiety.

Defining anger could take on many forms. One of my brothers is my complete opposite. He rarely gets upset by anything, and when he shows anger, he is over it easily. I didn't inherit that gene. My anger would be the strong passion of emotion that makes my displeasure known. The crazy thing is that anger doesn't have to be caused by a real event. It can be perceived to be real by an innocent situation. I know I can overanalyze and make myself the victim in any event.

I also used my anger to push people away. If I felt I was being pulled into doing something I didn't want to do, I would unload a whole boatload of vehement exasperation. A volcano would explode as all that was well within was just overcome by all that was not well. Believe me when I say there was a whole slew that was not well within. Using the volcano as an analogy for how I acted during this time, I can assure you that I had steam coming out of my ears. My face and neck would be red. My fists would be clenched and ready to deliver a punch if it was required to get my point across. The pressure was always within, always building, and when I blew, I spewed. Unlike my brother, I never got over it. It was always with me. I could remember any incident in which I was injured physically or emotionally, even if it was only a perceived wrongdoing. It consistently kept the underlying volcano active.

As stated at the beginning, I lived in the graveyard, going from tomb to tomb and lamenting all that had been done to me. I would take to time to stop at each tomb to relive the event of abuse, rejection, and accusations of wrongdoing in which I was innocent. I relived these things to the point of feeling the hurt, anger, and disappointments again. Day and night I was here, not allowing myself peace, but constantly opening wounds. Never healing, picking the scabs to bring back the bleeding. On to the next tomb, and repeat. Over and over again, new tombs were built, but the pathway was always worn between old and new. Nothing was ever left to rest. Therefore, I could not rest.

Not allowing closure to come to any wound was detrimental in many ways: The mental anguish of living in the tombs of wounds, always grieving, never flourishing in any way. Being constantly angry over events that were years old. I didn't want to forget, much less forgive. **The best lessons in life are the ones that were the hardest to learn.** Each of the wounds were what I thought of as lessons learned. Were they, or was that my bitterness and anger leading my thinking? The one who caused the wound most likely didn't have any recollection of the event. Hanging out in the tombs was a self-destructive habit. Even so, this was comfortable. It was scenery that I was used to. Did I want to leave? Sure. Did I know how? No. Not understanding what was outside of the graveyard made moving there unlikely. Could I remain here? Of course, it would always be my choice. Was the pain of staying in the graveyard, constantly in pain, crying out day and night what I wanted for the remainder of my days? Or was the pain of moving towards closing wounds the better choice? Either way, it was going to be painful. Leaving the graveyard meant the opportunity of finding life. Was it possible to be happy? To be content? All past experiences had shown that this was highly unlikely. Could I risk trying to leave the graveyard? To leave my anger behind? It was an intriguing thought — intriguing enough that it became a risk I was willing to take.

To allow healing would require movement towards the gate leading out. One tomb at a time, staring each one down, allowing myself to see it for what it was. Speaking forgiveness as needed. Did this mean confronting the one who wounded me? No. Forgiveness was not for them; it was all for my benefit. I know this sounds weird. Being angry with someone who doesn't know you are angry is crazy! **Realizing to the point of acceptance that humans are fallible and will unknowingly do harm surprisingly brings great peace.** Being stuck looking at a tomb, reopening it time and time again, brings about a tremendous smell. Let the rottenness go away. Stop reliving the pain. Does that mean you have to forget? No, it is not likely that you forget the bigger wounds, but you will not be controlled by the emotions that accompany that wound. For me, it meant my constant anger slowly diminished. This was not an overnight process. With some of the bigger events, I was urged to utilize a professional. I did not want to be one those people who went to counseling. Ugh. Now, I am one of their biggest fans. I often tell people, "You will love it. Being able to tell all your secrets and knowing that person cannot speak about it. And you will never see them again." Not seeing them again means no shame. Entrusting them with your deepest thoughts requires a trust that doesn't happen in the first session. For me, the trust grew as my need to share did. Stepping out, speaking, and hoping for the best only to realize that over the years some of the facts had become jumbled with my thoughts. I needed someone to assist me in seeing truths. Once the truth was out there, forgiveness became an easier task. Not easy, but easier and less stressful. The emotional distress was put into perspective that brought enlightenment to the depth of the wound. Understanding why I had held the wound so closely, which then brought the willingness to let go of the intense grip I had on it.

Forgiving others was easier than laying down my self-hatred. The dislike I had for myself would be best described as loathing. I hated every bit of my being. I hated myself so much that I abused myself with verbal assaults as well as self-beatings. I described my worth as being equal to a piece of garbage that was dumped on an abandoned road. Dumped to be forgotten, worthless, of no value to another. There is a Scripture that states that you should love our neighbor as yourself. I always scoffed and mumbled how sorry I felt for my neighbor. I was very aware that I didn't like myself, much less love myself. This self-hate was the basis of my discontent. I had never experienced unfailing love. I was certain that I never would. It was comfortable to hate myself and normal to hear a verbal onslaught. I once told my counselor that I was smart enough to not have kids so as not to continue the cycle. Her reply stunned me and made me stop to rethink my behavior. **Only a solid truth can stop one in their tracks like that.** She helped me see the cycle had not stopped. I may not have had a next generation, but I hadn't allowed the abuse to end in my life. I was continuing on with what I was taught. I only knew how stupid I was, or that my appearance wasn't acceptable, and neither was my behavior. I couldn't blame another this time. I wasn't someone's innocent victim. I was making the choice to continually beat myself down emotionally and beat myself up physically. Could it be that I really had something to offer? That I could be accepted? And that if I was rejected, it wouldn't be the end of the world? Was that really within my reach? Did I dare try?

It was clear that I had to try. I had to allow myself to see what was good in me. This was not easy. It required much effort; really, it was a major battle. I had to dig a foxhole and not be moved until I could move forward to the next foxhole. I slowly gained ground to find the place of self-acceptance and peace within with who I was. I tore down walls brick by brick. Each brick represented the hate I had toward my perceived stupid, ugly self. I replaced each brick with goodness. Look and see what the Lord has done. He turned this ugly, wretched being into someone who is full of joy. I can laugh at myself when I make a mistake. I don't require a self-beating to get myself back on track. I love myself enough to treat myself with respect, and I don't feel sorry for my neighbor. Am I perfect? Far from it. Accepting and perfect are different things. I accept who I am, in all of my human frailty. It is a wonderful place to be. Am I content with who I am? Never—I am always open to seeing my faults and working towards being a better me. **The difference now is that I don't hate the fault. I embrace my human frailty, knowing that change is possible even if it is unlikely.** It is certainly worth the effort to try.

Suicidal Thoughts

What's interesting is that my suicidal planning didn't go away with the self-acceptance. It stayed as one of my unhealthy coping mechanisms. It was frustrating. As I deal with depression, I am often asked if I have thoughts of suicide. I hated this question and usually would lie to the health professional asking it. In truth, there wasn't a day that went by that I didn't think about it, beginning when I was 16. It was embarrassing to be a follower of Christ and still battle depression and suicidal thoughts. The perception I had was that depression should have left with becoming a follower of Christ. It is an effort to put on a mask. Fellow Christians seem to rate sins, and it feels as if you can't be real about being depressed. Fake it until you make it, right? And who wants to hang out with Debbie Downer? My perception was that my depression made me a downer to be around.

My conversations with God boiled down to three statements:

1. I don't want to die.
2. You don't want me to take my own life.
3. What is the issue here?

It was obvious God and I had the same goal. Then why was I still planning suicides? I would pray for God to take this away. I memorized Scripture about choosing life. None of this was working. It eventually wasn't a struggle that overcame every thought in my head, but it was still frustrating. Years would pass without any relief from this thought pattern. I had learned not to give place to the planning part. I would battle back with the statement, "I don't want to do this and am choosing not to." Still, it would pop up at the most inconvenient times.

I didn't understand what I could do to battle this anymore. I really thought I was going to have to live the remainder of my life fighting these unwanted thoughts. I would openly discuss it with anyone who was willing to listen and not react by calling 911. I wore people out with it. I was accused of crying wolf too many times. This was not my intent. I was struggling with something that had a hold on me. I couldn't comprehend why. What more could I do to make it stop? Had it been such a part of me for so long that it would never go away? Maybe. I was a smoker for 16 years. As much as I know I don't want to return to that habit, I still have days when I want to smoke at 3 pm. Yes, I can tell you the exact time by when the craving hits. Why 3 pm? It came from when I worked with a group of smokers. We would take our afternoon break together at 3. During the break, we discussed the stresses of our day. Was it the cigarette I craved, or was it the companionship? Without a doubt it was the companionship.

So, what was it about these thoughts that was so seductive? If I am in control of my thoughts, then why couldn't I stop them? Having your mind overcome by unwanted thoughts means only dwelling on that thought. Breaking this incredibly irritating thought pattern would require a strategic battle plan. I began to note what was happening in and around my life at the time of the bombardment. Was it anything worth killing myself over? No. Then I had to look at the underlying theme of the past several days. It was only then that pattern began to reveal itself. As the stresses of life started piling up, I would begin to feel out of control. Who doesn't go through a phase of wondering how much more they can handle? For me when I hit the breaking point is the exact moment that the suicidal thoughts hit. Suicide planning had been a way of escape. My plan was never about how I could do it in the next 10 minutes — more like the next 10 weeks. Making the plan brought a sense of being in control, a place of calm and familiarity, even when the circumstances around me were out of my control. If I could plan when my life would end, then I would no longer have to deal with the uncontrollable surroundings. The fact that I never attempted a suicide, it is proof that the unbearable place I believed I was in didn't last as long as I anticipated.

This unhealthy coping mechanism started when I was a junior in high school. This was the second time my family had moved, the first being my freshman year. After 14 years in a small community, the move was not welcomed. As I started to adapt to the first move, it was announced that we were moving again. My brother was going into his senior year, so we stayed for him to graduate. My dad would be gone every week to where his new job was. The rest of us would follow at the end of the school year. Once I knew we were moving again, I stopped putting effort into relationships. What was the point? The second move had incredibly difficult circumstances. I was now in a school that had more kids in it than the town I grew up in. I didn't belong here. That's not a true statement. Of course, I belonged in the public school for where my home was. I didn't fit in here was the accurate statement. And I was never given a fair chance to fit in; I stood out as different, and I was alone. I couldn't walk through the halls without hearing the hateful words that pierce the heart. Day after day hearing insults, feeling hated. No place to turn, no safe refuge. It started on day one and steadily increased to the point of never walking the halls in peace. Gym class became a battlefield, with the locker room being a frightening place. I was often cornered with threats of physical violence. No teacher or classmate ever stepped in to stop it. This all gave me an inability to concentrate in the classroom. I was consistently writing in my notebooks three words: Help Me Please. No help ever came. My grades suffered tremendously. I was miserable.

When my junior year was over, I approached my parents about my senior year being back in my hometown. I had been offered a place to stay. I would be in a place where I wasn't hated every day. It was an incredible offer, and I wanted to take full advantage of it. My parents didn't agree. Their solution was for me to go to a private high school. Sure, changing schools again was the perfect answer. Not! Different hallways with different voices saying the same thing? To stay at the same school allowed me to have a familiar enemy. And I had managed to make a friend. I hated to give up that one friend.

Why was it so obvious I didn't fit in? Why were my classmates so full of hate? I can tell you that this is when I began to realize that I should have been male. I certainly wasn't comfortable as a female, and it showed in every way. Gender dysphoria or being transgender wasn't a topic at this time. Hate laws and anti-bullying campaigns were nonexistent. Nowhere to go, nowhere to hide, no place of acceptance to be found anywhere. My mother thought I was on drugs, as I came home in a different mood every day. My mood was based on how much hate I had endured that day. This was the environment they had chosen for me, so I didn't attempt to discuss anything with them. After all, everything was the result of what a stupid piece of crap I was, right? It was what I believed. The one constant in my life was being told I didn't have a brain and would never be successful. What's the saying? "Sticks and stones may break my bones, but words will never hurt me?" Ha. Words will last a lifetime. Words become sentences, and sentences become a story that defines the world around you, and even your own identity. They become a recording that repeats over and over in your head. It is always there until a different message is recorded over it.

I vividly remember the day I was shutting my locker and preparing to walk the hallway again. I leaned my head on the door, thinking that if only I could endure a little while longer, I would kill myself on my 25th birthday. I would have seen all I wanted to see by then. I would have done all I wanted to do. Why that birthday? I really do not have an explanation other than that it is a significant birthday in the scope of life. This was the birth of the unhealthy coping mechanism of suicide planning.

Suicidal Thoughts

I am over 25 years old, so it is obvious I didn't kill myself on that day. I did sit at the kitchen table late into the night. To do it or not to, that was the question. Much had changed about my circumstances. Life had been full of many events, good and bad. Were the good enough to keep going? Evidently so, as I am still here.

I had lived life with abandon. I had no fear of death and wanted it to come; I just didn't want it to occur as the result of an obvious action. I drove fast and recklessly. Alcohol became my best friend. Somehow it dulled the pain of life. I began to drink until I passed out. Soon that wasn't enough, and I added pain meds. I was drinking my way to a slow death. The day came when I was having significant chest pains. My nurse buddy in the ER hooked me up to a heart monitor. To the horror of both of us, the line went straight, and then my heart restarted on its own. She ran out of the room while I sat on the gurney in shock. She brought a doctor back with her and left us in the room together. He took a moment to look over the tape from the heart monitor. It only took him an additional moment to tell me that I would be dead by age 25. What wonderful news! I would succeed with my plan of being dead at the exact age I chose. However, this was not my reaction. I was 22, and for some reason, it wasn't an appealing way to die.

Choices were minimal then. I had sought help from a mental health professional, only to be denied. They wanted a sober client, and I couldn't imagine coping without a bottle. My fear of losing my job led to my going to rehab. Once again, my family didn't agree with my decision. I wasn't an alcoholic; therefore I didn't need rehab. At the same time, my body was used to the presence of alcohol. Stopping immediately required some assistance.

While in treatment, I spoke of being molested for the first time. I have to admit I was in one of the most dysfunctional facilities at the time, but I didn't have many options due to my rural location. It was the dead of winter, and I was ten miles from the nearest town. I begged my friends to come to my rescue. Each of them told me later how difficult it was to leave me there. I was stuck, and I had to find a way to make it work. The female leader I made my admission to was less than kind. She pointed out the obvious: that every female is molested at some point in her life. "Get over it" was her only advice. Wow, really? I had never spoken of this before. It was obviously a painful secret. Her response made me realize I should never speak of it again. I think the phrase is "Suck it up, buttercup." In my case, it was to make it another tomb in my graveyard.

Once I was discharged, I went to a professional counselor. I really wanted it to be my last. Nothing good came out of our time together. She inflicted additional injury to my recently opened wounds. Again, the message I received was "Get over it. You are not the only woman who has ever dealt with this." Seriously? It is a very sad fact that many women are molested in some way. As with any trauma, people deal with it in very different ways. Telling someone to just get over it minimizes what they have experienced. It was wrong of them to handle it this way. Their treatment of this would be considered unprofessional in the current climate. Their mishandling of the situation affected me deeply. The professional counselor suggested that I was in love with my friend and that I needed to make a life with her. Her voice nudged me towards the decisions I made in becoming involved with Grace.

I had now lost the way I numbed myself and promptly gave place to another unhealthy coping mechanism of dissociative behavior: a way of disconnecting with the current events of that moment in time. I will discuss this in greater detail in the next chapter. I'm sure it was a behavior I'd had for a long time, and it increased greatly at this time. I filled my evenings with sports activities and took a three-week vacation to Europe. Life wasn't fabulous, but it was doable. Was it doable because of being able to go elsewhere in my mind, my newest coping mechanism? Deep down, I was still miserable. I was taking it day by day and enjoying the good moments as they came, but they were quick to vanish. Was this all life had for me? Knowing I was being held captive in the wrong body kept me from dating; it kept me lonely. I didn't share my feelings. Who would understand, anyway?

Then life took an interesting turn. I made a new female friend, Grace. She didn't drink and had just moved to town. We didn't work the same shift, but yet we found time to take in the movies or explore new restaurants in the city. I felt she was being flirtatious at times, but I ignored it. I had no interest in being a lesbian. Then a night came when I was terribly sick. We were supposed to be spending time together that night, but my illness was not going to allow it. She wanted me to go to the hospital; I just wanted to go to bed. She argued that I shouldn't be left alone. I was too sick to care, and being alone was all I knew. I went to bed, only to be joined by her a few minutes later. It was at that moment that something inside of me changed. I had pressed these feelings down, believing I could never act on them. For the first time in my life, I felt like someone truly cared whether I woke up the next morning or not. I didn't know what to do—well, that's not true. I needed to sleep and feel better.

This night was a game changer for me. Would it be OK to accept her advances? Should I tell her how I really felt about being a trapped man? Taking one moment, one day at a time, we eventually became a couple. Shortly after that, we moved in together, renting a three-bedroom house, with each of us having a separate bedroom for appearances' sake. It was our desire to keep the semblance that we were just roommates. Life was good. I was happy and ready to settle in, but I was still longing for more, and it was the first time I believed I could have more.

We went on a weeklong cruise together. We were excited to get away from work, her family, and the small town we resided in. The weather was perfect, the seas reasonably calm. The ship had much to do, and the excursions were great experiences. We enjoyed ourselves immensely. However, this experience had an unexpected side effect for me. I had always wanted to be "normal." I didn't want a life where I had to hide anything. I wanted to be affectionate: a doting partner, a true gentleman, if you will. The week together had made it agonizingly apparent that our relationship was not within the parameters of what I deemed normal.

Not much more time passed before I finally decided to share my true desire with her. To speak and share thoughts that I hadn't dared to share before. Would she think I was crazy? Would she reject me and leave? Could I risk telling her? What would I do if she rejected me? Oh my goodness, could I make myself any crazier than I already felt I was? My mind swirled with every possible negative scenario. Why couldn't I be content with what we had?

It became glaringly obvious that I was withholding something from her. We had been together long enough that she could tell I was struggling with something. I had to tell her now. If I didn't, it would certainly lead to her being hurt by my choice not to talk. I began to fill her in with my belief that I was born the wrong sex and needed to have gender reassignment surgery. I wasn't a woman, but a man held captive in a female body. It didn't come out as smoothly as I have written it. My utterance was met with resounding silence, followed by uncomfortable silence. I left the room sick to my stomach. It was the first time in my adult life when I wanted to hide in a closet. I settled for sitting behind a chair and waiting for the expected rejection.

I'd been happy — why couldn't I have left things where there were? Why was I trying to get more? Within a few minutes, she came to the room I was in. She sat down and wanted to talk. She didn't look for me, only asked me to show myself so that we could talk. I was already thinking about the breakup and where I was going to move. Instead, she met me with love, compassion, and complete calm. Of course, she had been stunned by my words. She had needed a few minutes to absorb all that I had blurted out. Her next statements were words I didn't and couldn't expect to hear. She had been struggling with our relationship as well. She had no desire to be a lesbian, either. She had been grasping to understand her attraction to me all this time. She loved me; there was no doubt in that. Recognizing that I truly was in the wrong body made complete sense to her. I was relieved, happy, and too many other emotions to capture in words.

With the belief that I needed to proceed in changing my gender, we began to plan a future. I proposed, and she accepted. The wedding would be after my surgery. We needed to leave the small town we were in, and promptly picked the bigger city we would move to. We needed to become faces in a crowd instead of the faces the crowd was staring at. We needed to be able to find the health professionals who would assist me with my transition. Finally, I was going to be free to be what I believed I should be. Relief and excitement oozed out of me.

After the move, I began to cross-dress full time. We could finally go out on dates and proceed with normal couple activities. I eventually changed my name, and all was proceeding as I believed it should. Here is where I was on my 25th birthday: pursuing a life that I felt should have been all along.

Dissociative Behavior

As defined by Mayo Clinic, someone with a dissociative disorder escapes reality in ways that are involuntary and unhealthy. The person with a dissociative disorder experiences a disconnection and lack of continuity between thoughts, memories, surroundings, actions, and identity.[3]

Such a technical term for an unhealthy coping mechanism. I really had no idea that this was what my behavior was called, nor that it wasn't a normal activity for everyone. Somewhere in my adult life, I did begin to understand that it wasn't a behavior that everyone had. For me, it was a way to survive that was as natural as breathing. I named it "soap opera in my head," or "fantasy land." I always had a storyline going on in my mind. I could disappear from where I was physically located at any given moment and jump back into the story in my head. If I couldn't handle what was going on, my mind went to this safe place. It's hard to explain, and even harder to overcome. Some might argue that I was just daydreaming, but I'm not sure daydreaming has the amount of emotion attached to it that dissociative behavior does.

My storylines had a consistent theme and could last for weeks, months, or longer. In them, I was always male, with a wonderful personality. I was this terrific person who everyone wanted to be around. I always ended up married. Even though I was this terrific person, my wife became the exact opposite. In the beginning of my storyline, she was a normal, successful woman who was changing over time. She would become troubled in some way. I would have to be her rock and rescue her at a moment's notice. Of course, this made everyone else in my story adore me. How devoted I was, and incredibly patient. We would have children, and she was so dysfunctional that she couldn't tend to them. I had to do it, and the kids loved me for it. As these imaginary kids would grow, it would be required of me to explain why their mother was emotionally absent, making them love me even more for staying dedicated to her and never leaving her side. Eventually something would happen that would cause the story to turn violent. Every storyline ended with my death, and I always died in a gruesome way. It was never accidental, as I was brutally murdered. Then a new story would begin with all new characters. None of them was ever real or built around people I knew. The scenery was always a place I had lived at some point in my real life.

To look deeply at my storylines, it was always apparent how completely different my actual self was from the pretend self. The obvious one is easily identified, as I was male, not female. The next difference was in my basic personality traits: patient, even-keeled, and lovable. My real persona was a hot-headed, hate-filled tyrant. He was capable; I was inept. He was successful; I was a failure, and everything I laid my hands on became a complete disaster. The biggest difference was that he begged to live at each murderous moment, and I wanted to die every waking second. I can see why some may consider it a daydream. It was everything I wanted to be that was out of my reach, or at least that I believed I could never have.

By the time I admitted to this behavior, I was well into my adult life. It had served me well in a variety of situations. It got me through lonely nights, allowing me to escape into a world of being surrounded by people. This was definitely a place I could not be in real life. I often wondered how people could go to social situations without a care in the world. I would need to have consumed liquid courage and been given a script to tell me what to say once I got there. By the way, I was a fun drunk. Being drunk all of the time allowed me to be something I wasn't. My inhibitions were gone, but any intelligence I had went with it. Even as a drunk, I couldn't handle reality and made everything into a joke. That's why I perceived that I was loveable. Was I, or were people secretly seeing through the facade I was presenting?

If I found myself in an unwanted situation, I completely disappeared mentally, leaving my body void of any emotion. I didn't go anywhere physically. There was a shell of a human being there, one who didn't respond to any stimuli. You might be able to talk me back to the present, but patience was required. This was frequent if I somehow managed to get into a compromising situation. It was the only time I ever exhibited this behavior when I was in the company of a fellow human being. Obviously, this would freak out my companion, and all activities would cease. This was not an intended behavior, nor an anticipated one. Frankly, I didn't understand it, nor would I even attempt to explain it. I didn't know what to take away from it. It added to my silence, as I wouldn't even know how to share it. Needless to say, I never saw that person again, so I wasn't forced to dwell on what happened.

It can be such a wonderful thing to stick your head in the sand and ignore reality. Ignorance is bliss, right? **But I have learned that avoidance is a dance that doesn't get you anywhere.** It is exhausting to always be on the dance floor for those marathons. To come to the realization that it was not normal to be dissociative, then to admit it took a deeper level of courage that was new to me. **My desire to be whole had to increase as my pride decreased.** Maybe pride doesn't sound like the correct word. In essence, it is. Admitting that you need help is rarely easy. To admit to "crazy" behavior isn't something anyone wants to do. I mean, come on, if you know you have a crazy family member, you don't invite your friends to your house for a visit, do you? Who wants to put crazy on display?

Admitting this behavior required reaching deep inside to turn my gut inside out then pull it out, without getting sick, to verbalize something I didn't understand. Hey! Guess what? I escape reality at any and every opportunity I can. And sometimes I even leave when I am unaware I'm going to. Woo-hoo! Not. It was with great patience that I was simply asked what would be the hardest coping mechanism to stop using. We won't get into how many I actually had. I answered this simple, very compassionate question with, "Do you think I'm stupid?" I knew if I was being asked that question, the following one would be, "What would it take to not utilize it?" It may not be healthy, but I was certainly not going to give it up. It had served me well — or had it?

Once again, I was in the place of admitting I had a behavior that needed to change. To slip away into nowhere was easy to overcome: simply stop being in a compromising situation. Ok, easy enough. Give up any physical touch with another human. You can shake my hand, but no hugs allowed. Easy, I already had my wall around me that was five bricks deep. To willingly stop going away to fantasy land? Oh, take my breath away and say it isn't so! But as I stated in my objective at the beginning of the book, I wanted to be whole. To be whole required changes that were beyond painful.

I had many sleepless nights as I tried to stay present. As my mind would begin to slip away, I would have to make the choice to stay "home." To stay home meant dealing with the stressor that was making fantasy land so desirable. Yuck. It was time to grow up, to leave the childish thinking behind. To develop the skills that should have come while I was becoming an adult. Just because you get older doesn't mean that you think like an adult. I often joke that I am never going to grow up, that I am going to have childlike behavior for the remainder of my life. Enjoying throwing water balloons is completely different from learning adult cognitive skills. Instead of pretending I didn't have stress, I needed to learn how to deal with it, to learn to verbalize how I was feeling. Most importantly, I needed to develop problem-solving skills.

To overcome dissociation was a battle that was not won easily. It required tons of writing in a journal and time reading the journal to see if I could find the issue that was leading to the desire to dissociate. What I learned was that it was many issues. Great focus was demanded from me. I had to stay on task and never let my guard down to allow my mind to wander. I had spent a lifetime drifting into another world. To not drift meant to stay alert, and this alertness didn't come with drinking coffee. I had to post a guard at the entrance to my mind and be selective about what I allowed to enter, and somehow still function in the real world as the stress built and the sleepless nights piled up.

To give in would have been easy. To quit was an option that I wouldn't entertain. It was one hour at a time. Then maybe an entire day. Would two days in a row ever be a reality? Once two happened, could three? How about a week? To say I built momentum would be a lie. Each hour was battle, a choice. To slip meant going backwards many steps. The slips did occur, and they were disheartening. Frustration mounted, but determination became my backbone. My newest phrase was "Determination until I reach the destination." What was the destination again? To have peace and be free from torment. To be in a storyline where the ending was always violently traumatic was not peaceful, nor free from torment. Couldn't I make the story end a different way? Strangely enough, no. This had been years in the making. To change the ending wouldn't take away the root of the issue. The behavior had to stop. It was unhealthy as well as not useful for living life to its fullest.

I can't tell you how many years it has been since I stopped dissociating. I didn't mark it on the calendar when I realized the battle had been won. I never wanted to let my guard down, thinking, daring to believe I had won. Somewhere in there, I did. I have been tempted to go "away" again. It just doesn't have any appeal to it—to be present in this day, in this moment, to take it all in. Good and bad, I would rather be able to deal with the stresses as they occur, compared to avoiding them until I am drowning. I wanted a life worth living. I found that, and I want to stay in the reality of it. **Troubles will come, but they do not define me. They will not overtake me.** I learned the appropriate skills needed to deal with life. The use of these skills has removed my desire and need to dissociate.

Crossdressing Years

Such an interesting term. I can understand why it is used, but seriously, folks. To dress in clothes traditionally worn by the opposite sex. That is how you see it, but not how I did. It was a step in the guide for those seeking sex reassignment surgery. Now the more politically correct words are *gender reassignment*. It is a confusing world that takes an open mind to completely understand. I am not taking on the task of explaining terms, as they will change again someday. As a person who believed that I was born the wrong sex/gender, it was natural to wear men's clothing. Why was it termed cross-dressing then? According to the manual that I used in the mid 80's, it was a requirement to dress as the sex/gender that you were pursuing. I am laughing out loud as I type the word *pursue*. To define pursue is to strive to gain; seek to attain or accomplish. Striving to gain something that I believed that was actually correcting a wrong. On the other hand, it was something I was trying to accomplish. It was meant as a trial run to help you make sure it was indeed what you wanted to do. For me, it was a welcomed opportunity.

To get up every morning and take the time to look male was a chore. My wardrobe needed to hide the binder of my chest. I worked in a dress shirt and tie, so the undershirt helped immensely. I found men's clothing to be much more comfortable and functional. I never felt like it was a charade or like I was pulling the wool over people's eyes. This was a way to feel normal for the first time in my life. I'm sure gay bars were around at the time, but that isn't how I saw myself. I stayed in the mainstream of restaurants and movie theaters, as well as every other place. I wanted a mustache, so I went to a theatrical store to purchase one. It was great until it fell off at dinner in a crowded restaurant. I loved to laugh at myself during this time in my life. It was trial and error to see what worked and what was a complete failure. Presenting myself as a male didn't seem to be questioned by anyone. I felt at ease and accepted for the first time in my life.

The next natural step was to change my name. This was simple enough. Appear in court, run an ad in the paper stating the change. Then taking the court documents to all of the appropriate government facilities to get all of those names updated. It was not a question what letter was put next to Sex. I now had a male name, and therefore it was an M. Just like that, I was considered to be male by the government. The best laugh I had was when my car insurance rates went up because of the name change. My driving record had nothing to do with it. I was now in the category of a higher insurance risk. I couldn't argue it, but still. My medical insurance had the opposite approach. I stayed female in their opinion. Of course, this meant I had higher premiums as well. Once again, I couldn't argue with the logic. I still had all my female anatomy and needed to have the corresponding coverage. To be honest, I do not know how my primary care doctor had me listed in my chart. This was all in the stone age, when you weren't given internet access to your records.

In order to complete my wardrobe, I even bought a suit and had it tailored to fit. It is amazing how many times you can wear the same suit by changing up the shirt. Anyway, even this process was accomplished without drama. It's easy for people to look at me now and question that I was successful in my endeavor. In order to help convince you, I will bring you into a relationship in my life that was business casual. I had a small business I ran besides my full-time job. I would often go to meetings to learn the trade. It was the usual crowd at the majority of these meetings. Over time, I met a couple I would speak to every time we crossed paths. No questions asked, just a laid-back non-meaningful conversation. Often these meetings would be regional, which obviously meant they were bigger. After I began to pursue God and made the abrupt change back to my biological gender, I still attended these meetings. People higher up the food chain were aware of what was going on. They encouraged my pursuit of God and the steps I was taking, but when I saw this couple, their reaction was different. He stepped back and wouldn't shake my hand. Instead, he shook his head and voiced his disgust with who I was as a human being. That is not the reaction of a man who had any inkling that I was a female dressed in male clothing.

I had met others along the way who accepted me as male. Unfortunately, I had someone who felt it should be known that I wasn't who they thought I was. This was a very spiteful woman who was out to destroy someone else by using the knowledge she had about me. She wasn't in my inner circle, where I had built a relationship. I'm not sure who she was looking to hurt by telling people about me. Even so, I saw it as violation. The result was the same. All of the sudden, I was not welcome. Opinions were shared in harmful ways. Disgust. I was a perfectly acceptable person until they found out I wasn't wearing the clothing that they deemed appropriate. Wow. Can you say painful? The worst part was that I didn't have a clue that they had been given this knowledge. I wasn't prepared for the verbal onslaught that came in what I believed was a safe place. Understanding was not sought out. Rejection was the only offer on the table.

The recurring theme in my life was that people were not trustworthy. I had little to no value to offer them as a fellow human. I was expendable. I am still perplexed at how I was welcomed and accepted until my private life was announced. I wanted to be mainstream, to fly under the radar. I desired a normal life. Regardless of my outward appearance, I am still the same person. My character didn't change. The person I was — my views, humor, quiet nature, or anything else about me — didn't change. What did change was the others' ability to see me as a human being. They forgot why they liked me or hung out with me. All they could see was something that they had an issue with. And of course, this was followed by their need to tell me how much they objected to what I was doing. As a result of the hate I had received in my life, my only expectation of other humans was to be rejected and hated.

It wasn't the first of the many lessons that people will fail me. Depending on another for internal happiness is a dangerous place to be. For me to be accepted by them, I needed to meet the requirements that they had in mind for me. There wasn't love and acceptance, or "Let me stand next to you to help you see that there may be a different path." It was vile, spiteful words. Have you ever noticed that vile and evil have the same letters in them? Am I saying they were evil? Perhaps I am insinuating that. I can say without a doubt that they were not charming or without fault in their actions. Whether or not they meant to spew hatred at me, that was certainly the result. I am a firm believer that actions speak louder than words. Their actions were undeniable in showing contempt.

What I find most disturbing about these interactions is that these people self-identified themselves as Christians. At the time this was transpiring, I really did not give it any thought, and as my life went on, I never looked back and thought about these people. Their point had been made, and the relationship terminated. Today when I reflect upon this, I am grieved by their actions. Not for the way they wounded me, but for the way they presented them-selves: high-and-mighty people declaring to the world that they are representatives for Christ. It is seen all too often in our current climate. So often that I am leery of answering questions asking if I am a Christian. I'm certainly not perfect, but I hope that I can have a conversation to gain understanding. **The one thing I am confident in is that I am not the Judge — none of us are.**

I was more than willing to lose friends during my journey. I wasn't living my life to please them or anybody else. I was following my feelings and doing what I needed to do to feel comfortable in my own skin. As I was a fair person, I always listened to the hatred being thrown at me. I would take it to heart, carry it into my home, and cry. Why was life so hard? Why did people have to express their opinions in such harmful ways? What was so wrong with me? It's ironic that I thought the problem was me. Really, the issue was with the hater. Why couldn't anyone sit down, talk, and try to gain understanding? That was too hard. It is easy to be a hater. I never returned hate for hate. I absorbed it, expected it, and ultimately became numb to it.

I continued to move on in my journey. In this decade, hormones would not be administered until you completed twenty-four months of cross-dressing. I'm certain that isn't the case today, but I am not educated about it. To be honest, I haven't looked at what is required, as my belief is that if you have cash, you will find someone willing to supply you with what you need. For me, the thought of receiving hormones meant that I could finally grow a real mustache. My voice would get deeper, even though I wasn't having an issue with my current voice. Once on hormones, I could plan the double mastectomy and bid goodbye to binding my chest forever. I was looking at spending a minimum of $50,000 just for the surgeon. A small price to pay for happiness, right? I was blinded by what I thought would bring me to a place of contentment. Being at peace and happy.

Turning away from the pursuit to have the surgery was a decision made in a few days, but the changes required to accept being female were years in the making. Can you repeat that? It's a way of saying that the mind was willing to follow what I believed God wanted. My emotions were not in the same place. Just because I stopped wearing men's clothing didn't change my inward being. My appearance became a little more feminine, but I didn't immediately begin wearing dresses and putting on makeup. Again, the transformation did not happen overnight. I had to place my feelings inside of my non-decision-making box. I purposely had to find someone to take me shopping to find clothes that helped me look feminine. At the same time, I had to be comfortable in them, or they were just going to hang in the closet.

I had a brother get married during the time when I did not communicate with my family. When I finally met his wife, one of the questions she had for me was whether I liked dudes now. This is a question that took guts to ask, and probably one my entire family wanted the answer to. Surprisingly, I still get asked it today, so there are many who think it is relevant. My desire to change my gender was never about who I was attracted to. As I said, I had no interest in being a lesbian. My thought process was that I was born the wrong sex; therefore, I should change it and proceed with life accordingly. I wasn't changing my sex in order to fit my attraction. Nor did I immediately go look for a man to be with when I stopped pursuing the surgery. I was too busy trying to figure out how to get through each day of my life, with everything being different from all of my previous years.

Nobody seems to be content with accepting that who I was attracted to wasn't the most important thought in my head at the time. Somewhere in the midst of everything that was happening, I had the realization that I needed to get my life straight before I allowed anybody intimately into my life. I wasn't looking for any person to fill a space in my life. This is when I began the pursuit of wholeness. Not becoming dependent on another for my happiness, to be rescued and have every moment depend on that person. Been there, done that, and realized I deserved better than that. Did the desire to date a male happen? Yes, it did, and I have been on dates. To try to figure out exactly when I decided it would be appropriate to date is an absurd thing to do.

Nature vs. Nurture

I love being a part of this debate. Not! It is my personal belief that so many people have asked homosexuals why they are attracted to the same sex that the answer became "I was born this way." Does anyone really have an understanding as to why they are the way they are? Genetics continue to be researched in many ways. I can remember my biology class talking about the chances of people having blue eyes or red hair. Your genes are what they are. There are many diseases that are believed to be genetic, proven by the fact that doctors want to know your family history. Scientists will continue to research every facet of our being until the end of time.

Then you have the people who believe that everyone who is a homosexual was sexually abused as a child. Wow. What a hardcore line to put on to people. Is that a way of saying if you would just get over the trauma of having your body violated, you could be attracted to the opposite sex? The statistics of how many children are abused is staggering. Then if you compare it to the small proportion of the population that is homosexual, your belief should be blown out of the water right there. It is a narrow-minded person who doesn't want to see anything further. It is a painful assumption to be the recipient of.

To be put in a place of having to explain myself isn't a place I wanted to be. When I came to the self-realization that I was born the wrong sex/gender, I didn't announce it in the papers. I quietly kept it to myself. Just as with someone who is born without a limb, adapting to life the way it is becomes important. In college, I had a blind friend who was utterly amazing. She never once saw her lack of sight as a burden. Never experiencing the spectrum of colors of a sunset was not a concern in her mind. She adapted to the life that she was in. This is what I tried to do as well. I was born a female and did my best to live that life. I had a steady boyfriend throughout college. I went on girls' weekends into the mountains. I didn't have any sisters, and was generally considered a tomboy. Nobody accused me of being a homosexual just because I was rough-and-tumble and preferred to play football with the boys. I never considered myself to be a homosexual. That is a label that others chose to put on me.

Was it my nature to have the desire to be male, or was it my childhood influences that caused it? Can you see the silliness of the debate? If you blame it on my childhood, are you blaming my parents and brothers, or the way I responded to my circumstances? My childhood best friend and I were inseparable. We played with army men that were transported in my Barbie camper and Tonka trucks in the sandbox. In junior high, we both wanted to try out for football. After I had moved, I dropped in on her unexpectedly during our high school years. She came to the door in a dress, with makeup on. She was getting ready to go out on a date. I had to take a second look, as I didn't recognize my friend. We were both tomboys, yet she went on with a traditional life. "Traditional" according to the model of expectations that are placed on young people: graduate, go to college, get married, and have a family of your own.

If you say I was born that way, then are you blaming God for my genetics? As I was living my life, I can assure you that this was not a question I lost any sleep over. In fact, I am certain I never even gave it a minute of my time. Why do we need to know the reason for everything? When does acceptance start? Understanding, kindness, and implementing the golden rule of treating others as you want to be treated?

Nature Vs. Nurture

At age 22, when I was sitting on the gurney watching my heart stop, it didn't matter that I was female or male. What mattered was that I was living a life that meant I needed to self-medicate. I didn't understand why. I could only tell you that I had a hard time in daily life. One of my go-to statements was "Life is hell. If you do right in this life, then you get to go to heaven. If you screw up, then you are sentenced to do it all again." This from an atheist, who didn't believe in God, and therefore couldn't believe in heaven or hell. It was the only way I could wrap my mind around a life that was wandering aimlessly. I had no sense of purpose, and no hope of better days ahead.

When I began to cross-dress, and pursue the surgery, life became more bearable. It felt comfortable and right in a way I had never had before. The obvious question should be, did that contentment come from having a mate that really loved me? Or was it because I was starting to feel comfortable in my own skin? One thing that is for sure is that I had never relaxed in the belief that I was wanted before this time, but my inner struggles were still brewing underneath the surface. I had the belief that Grace wanted to be with me, yet I would put her to the test often in ways that required her prove her loyalty over and over. Why couldn't I accept it? Why did I need these reassurances all of the time?

It would be an accurate statement that I didn't feel loved or accepted as a child. My anger issues were evident at a young age. This leads many to the assumption that my actions were a result of my nurturing. I really take offense that people outside of my home want to blame my family. Was my life perfect? What's perfect in reality? Most people I know would say there was dysfunction in their childhood homes. How much the dysfunction affected them as compared to their siblings varied in significant ways. Does this blow the nature theory completely? Evidently not, as it is a topic of conversation that seems to still exist.

If you saw a family photo, you would know that my brothers and I look similar. My friends often comment on my pictures about that very fact. So, can it be genetic, nature? They are all in heterosexual relationships. I seriously doubt any of them every even had a thought about being female. Looking up and down my extended family, there isn't anyone else who had my thoughts. This brings me to the point: How can it be genetic?

As I have opened up about my life to many people over the years, I have been asked why I thought I did what I did. It makes me chuckle every time. I am not looking for the answers that outsiders are. My focus was always on what I needed to do to overcome any obstacle that was between where I was and the place of wholeness that I was pursuing. Trying to decide whose fault it was? Never a concern.

Expectation of Rejection

I've often thought that a serial killer would be more loved than someone who was categorized under the umbrella of being a homosexual, as long as that killer was a heterosexual. People have long been intrigued by criminals and looked into their personal history to see what might be behind their actions. You can find documentary after documentary on criminals. Interviews of family and friends who either knew that they would be what they became or were shocked by their actions. You rarely will find a documentary on the victim, nor the tragedy that was left behind. That doesn't sell. There is a lack of empathy for the survivors, but a strange attraction to the one who committed heinous acts. Of course, these shows are produced after the perpetrator is safely behind bars and can't hurt us. However, the survivors are easily forgotten as we go on with our daily lives. Even if the killers weren't locked up, if they walked into a room, I am certain that they wouldn't expect anyone to rush over to meet them. Their crimes have been splashed throughout the headlines. Their life has been dragged through the images in the press. They have been made out to be animals, subhuman or nonhuman. There would be stares out of the corner of everybody's eyes. Murmuring, questioning why they are there and would show their face in public. If this continued on for years, the killer would eventually expect rejection.

To reject is to refuse to accept, to discharge as useless or unsatisfactory. Most of society would have a hard time accepting the killer into their lives. As a person who didn't seem to fit into my surroundings, ever, I too often had perceived rejection. I came to reject the expectation that anyone I met would try to befriend me or try to understand my actions. My parents had never tried to understand me, so why would anyone else? **I was so hurt by the world that I could not risk opening myself up to anyone ever again.** Even if someone had approached me gently with simple questions, I would have been too skeptical of their motives. I knew I was unlovable. I wanted to be left in peace to live my life.

Having an outward issue that isn't considered to be socially normal for some reason set a target on me. Whether or not I was acting on it had no bearing on the matter. To find acceptance was never an expectation. It is a fact that most people are friends with people they have something in common with. It brings a sense of comfort. A knowledge that you aren't going to be hated just for being in the room. Eventually, isolation from everything else starts to happen. The pain takes over, and the need for safe refuge is all that matters. Feelings trump facts. Because rejection happened from one person, I in turn expected it from their entire family. The more you sink into the refuge, the more you isolate yourself from the remainder of the world. Somehow that isn't enough. The hate still finds its way into your shelter.

It's no wonder the world is full of groups that have been labeled. It is a wonder that anyone leaves their comfort zone to interact with another. Some who do are so hard-skinned that they just don't care about making another uncomfortable. Others want to seek out those they have differences with just to broaden their views. In turn, they may find a true gem of a person who has been unwilling to interact because they are controlled by the fear of rejection.

I have said many times that the unfortunate thing about being categorized under the homosexual umbrella is that it is generally worn on the outside for people to see. A serial killer doesn't wear a sign around their neck that says, "I like to kill people." I played softball with a group of women for several summers. I will never forget when an openly gay teammate stated that another teammate was gay, and she just didn't know it yet. Really? Was that an accurate statement? Or a hopeful one? Homophobes often believe that gay people want to be in a romantic relationship with them. My answer to that would be "Get over yourself. Are you kidding me? This makes it all about you. Your fear is controlling you, and really has nothing to do with the other person. To be blunt, this may be your need to be in control by keeping away people you don't agree with."

I was so conditioned to believe that I couldn't really be wanted that it drove me to consistently test Grace. The fact was, I expected her to reject me until it finally happened. Did I drive her to it? Maybe in some small way, I did. I don't overanalyze what happened at the end of our relationship too much. I do realize that if I had been in a heterosexual relationship, I would have had the same behavior. I had a plethora of experiences that were affecting my daily life. Some I remembered, others I didn't.

The expectation of rejection limited my life. It brought tremendous anxiety into any social setting. Even time with family, pre-cross-dressing, during it, and certainly after. I couldn't relax or allow myself to let my fun personality show. Before I stepped into a room of strangers, I knew it was going to be awful. The fear drove my actions. How long do you want to talk to someone who won't make eye contact or only gives one- or two-word answers to your questions? I was trembling inside, which caused my brain to freeze. I was unable to enter into a conversation that I may actually have enjoyed. My only thought was how fast I could get out of there.

I couldn't believe it when I finally put together that it was my expectations that were causing me to not be able to expand my network of friends. I realized that I had hindered myself, and it wasn't the other people. Were they judging me? No, they weren't; it was my fear driving my beliefs. Did life get better when I understood my shortcoming? You bet it did. I was still socially awkward; that didn't go away, as I had never had a chance to build these skills before I was controlled by my fear. It took time to talk my fear away, to trust what was said to me and not what I thought. I needed to have awareness of the reality of the situation and to stop leaning on my perception. My feelings are dangerous and can lead me astray.

It amazes me how easy it was to be afraid of rejection, especially when I think about how expansive this fear was; it covered my every thought. I mean seriously to believe that if your sibling didn't like me, that meant that I wouldn't even give you a chance to know me or for me to know you. It is heartbreaking to be on the side of seeing a friend not in communication with their family because of the choice made by a different one of their siblings. Because one of them takes issue with your life, doesn't mean they all do. To step out and take a chance that you could be involved with a different member? Can that be done? It's a risk, but isn't the chance worth it? Family will stand by you when others won't, or family will throw you down the drain and close every door, which is their loss. Each of us has something wonderful to give to others. Look for the ones who want you for you, not because they can control you to make you what they want you to be. You may find that one sibling who is entirely different than the outspoken one. Wouldn't it be incredible to find out that they don't have the thoughts about you that you think they do? Go for it; you've got nothing to lose that you don't already think is lost.

Repressed Memories

I would rather chop off my hands than have this experience again. I am not a scholar, and therefore have not studied the theories behind when memories are easily remembered and when they are buried from the conscious mind. My only attempt is to explain how this affected my life, good and bad. It is a time in my life that I do not wish upon another. It is confusing beyond all measure.

First, I had to do everything possible to live in the present. Second was trying not to let the memories of the past affect the current moment. The final thing was trying to make sense out of the memories that were forcing their way into my life. To say I felt crazy would be an understatement. I'm not sure how I got out of bed to have a functional life. I've always said I couldn't have done it without God in my life. Each day I faced triggers that caused the memories to flood my mind. There weren't words that could express what was happening: confusion, terror, and heartbreak all at once.

To think it all started on a day I was reading a book. A flash of a picture from my childhood bedroom went through my mind. I remember pausing to try to figure out what just happened. Nothing. I went on with my daily life. Then again, a few months later: another flash. These flashes were maybe three seconds in length. Just long enough to be noticed, but not so long that I could gain any understanding as to what I was seeing. Weird, right? Several months later, it happened again. I could place the scenery of my room, but nothing else in the brief moment made any sense.

About a year later, I was starting to have much longer flashes of this memory. I was no longer comfortable with ignoring these flashes, yet not sure how to proceed. Bewildered, I finally opened up to a friend about it. We talked about what I was seeing and how these moments had gone from seconds to almost a minute. Yet I had no directions as to what I could or should do about it. I wasn't seeing anything that was concerning. It was more of an interruption and something that I had no control over. To say I was scared wouldn't be accurate. However, it wasn't much longer before I began waking up to horrible nightmares. Now I was troubled as to what was happening. I was no longer just having short flashes during the day. It was turning into minutes of scenery that I couldn't deny were familiar. Once I could grasp that the scenery was accurate, I felt that I had to take notice of the events that were happening in the intrusive thought. As soon as I started to allow myself to analyze the picture before me, a different one appeared. Again, the scenery was real. I couldn't deny that, as much as I wanted to. Now I wasn't just scared—I was terrified.

Time went on, and the flashes increased. I eventually had to accept that these were events that I had no memory of. I didn't want what I was seeing to be real. I was sickened by what I was seeing, accompanied by emotions that I can't explain. But, if I was emotional over the picture, did that make it a real event? It couldn't be real. I didn't want it to be real. Slowly, I found myself in full-blown memory recall. I didn't like what I was seeing. I didn't want any of it to be true. But I was starting to gain an understanding as to why I had struggled throughout most of my life. Could any of this be true? I didn't want it to be. It was a horrible time to be stuck in the memories stalking my current life. I stopped talking to anyone about it. If I didn't talk about it, then maybe it would all go away. Alas, this didn't work. The stress was building. This wasn't something I could laugh my way through.

I began to refer to it as my closet day. This was the day that began a story that I hadn't remembered for thirty-some years. I often think of all the houses one will see on any city block. All of them have stories, with who knows how many closets. Closets full of skeletons. Skeletons waiting to be dealt with, waiting for the story to be told. As long as the door to the house is closed, the closets don't need to be opened. If the closets stay closed, the skeletons stayed hidden. I had a closet with a big ol' scary skeleton. It would seem as if I was being pressed into telling the story. At the very least, I had to acknowledge that the skeleton existed, to give it a voice to be heard.

I was wrestling with the idea of sharing. What I was seeing was sickening. It certainly wasn't dinner table conversation. Where would I start? I had little understanding of what I was seeing. I only knew that it was something I couldn't deny. As days passed, the memories grew. I saw myself hiding in the closet, with no understanding of why I was there. I asked God for understanding, and I then began to be haunted by another memory, then another. Would it stop? How much happened that I didn't remember? I felt fear, overwhelming anxiety, and a complete inability to control my mind. I'm so thankful for the few who stood by me during this time. I was incapable of being a good friend to anyone. I was self-absorbed in a trauma that was years old but felt like it was reoccurring every day.

Each day I left my home, I was guaranteed to be triggered into a flashback. I would react when anything significant happened quickly and unexpectedly to my left side. Of course, the opening of my work cubicle was on my left. I had a coworker that thought she was hysterical when she would jump into my cubicle to scare me. I would sit at my desk and cry, as I was so upset but did not have any real understanding as to why. What was happening to me? I couldn't go to a crowded store, as panic would set in. I could no longer be in any crowd at all. The fear of being attacked consumed me. I wasn't safe anywhere — or so I believed. It was hard to work through this fear. The chances that I was going to be attacked in a grocery store aisle were not realistic. In my mind, it was a risk to get trapped anywhere within the store. If I needed a canned good and that aisle had two people in it, I went home without that item.

You can't imagine how thrilled I was when a new grocery store opened up in my suburb where the aisles were wider than in any store I had ever been in before.

Work and back home, completely controlled by fear that I couldn't understand. My hideaway of sleep wasn't even safe anymore. I eventually began to use this to my benefit by going to the local 24-hour grocery store when I was the only shopper. For some unknown reason, I felt safe being out and about in the dark and alone, when I didn't have to share the space with anyone else. To be in a large store without seeing another being still had stress, as I was away from the safety of my home, but it allowed me to be enough at peace to gather my entire list. I often had to look for a clerk to check me out when I was ready.

I'm still amazed that I was able to go to work daily. I just happened to work in a secured building with security guards. I don't know if that helped me or not. I did treat work as a requirement in my life. Nobody else was going to pay my bills. I was still capable, therefore I worked. It beat the alternative of being homeless without the safety of a home.

Finally, the day arrived when I agreed to tell the story, to speak of the hideous things I was seeing. I opened the door to my house, the core of my being, to allow another in and leading the way to the closet to open the door and let the skeleton out: the whole story as I could see it at that moment. I withheld no details, even though I wanted to vomit as I was speaking them. By the end, I was doubled over and uncontrollably crying. Not just a few tears: enough to fill a big bucket. My counselor sat quietly as I sobbed. I had doubled over until I found myself on the floor, and all the while, the tears continued to pour out. As I finally caught my breath and calmed myself, I couldn't even look at her. I was so ashamed about what had happened to me. I didn't expect any compassion. After all, hadn't I gotten what I deserved? I was a worthless excuse for a human.

She stayed silent, waiting for me to compose myself enough to be able to look up at her. It was then that I saw her face. I saw the pain she was feeling for me. I was overwhelmed by the compassion I could see she had for me. There was no contempt. She wasn't telling me I was a liar. I spoke first: "It can't be true, right?" Her answer brought the tears back: "There was nothing made up that could conjure up that much emotion." Oh my, it is real! Now I really am going to vomit. How did I survive this attack? How could God have allowed me to go through that? What would it take to stop the flashbacks? Was it even possible to stop them? There was so much to take in. I felt ill-equipped to handle what lay in front of me. Would I ever be whole, or was all of this too much to overcome?

Month by month went by as the calendar turned over into a new year. For every three steps of progress that I made, I fell back two. It was a grueling process. I often believed it was just too much to overcome. I had been tortured, beaten, and left for dead: a three-part attack. I was angry at God for not allowing me to die during or even after the attack. I counted a minimum of three different ways I should have died. Why was I still here? My life had been full of suffering. Wouldn't a compassionate God have allowed me to go Heaven? Here I was having to fight for what I believed to be what a healthy, normal person was. Nothing came easy. Would determination until I reached the destination be enough resolve to get me through? My faith often wavered until I came back, hoping God would help me. Each time, He greeted me with open arms and held me as I wept through the pain of the healing. The pain of the transformation. **Just as a caterpillar becomes a butterfly, it must fight its way out of the cocoon. I too had to fight my way through the walls of protection I had built to keep harm out.** But those walls were also keeping anything positive out. What felt like protection was actually going to limit growth and healing.

In a strange turn of events, God began to slow the flashbacks down. I began to see them as a gift instead of torment. To be allowed to hear what was being said to me. To hear my thoughts to all that was happening. To gain understanding of where the self-hatred came from. Why I had such low self-esteem. The self-hating self-talk had been beaten into me during this attack. With each blow had been words of hatred. I literally had it beaten into me. After the torture, I had very little energy to try to defend myself. The beating had been brutal, but the words spoken to me were not forgotten like the attack was. My entire life had been filled with the memory of my worthlessness.

To be left for dead has few words to put to it. Really, I am not sure the concept of dying was there when I was a child. It was more the reality of not having any fight left in me. As I don't recall the moment this happened; I can only tell of what happened during the memories in the flashbacks, and the slow-motion ones at that. After the brutal attacks, I heard a voice calling me. A voice telling me I would be safe if I followed it. In my exhausted and broken state, I somehow managed to get to where the voice was by slowly crawling my way across the ground to pull myself into the closet, where there was seemingly a line drawn that my attacker could not cross. I soon learned that the voice belonged to Jesus. When I arrived, I had a brief moment when I was on my hands and knees. I stopped briefly to observe the amount of blood on me and what was dripping from my wounds. I then collapsed into His lap. He held me and tended to every wound, nursing me back to health. What a picture to hold onto, not just for me, but for everyone. At that moment in my actual life, my needs were to have my physical wounds attended to. At the time of seeing this in my flashbacks, it was time to allow Jesus to tend to all of my emotional wounds. To hold me, give me the courage to go forward. The strength to get up each day, knowing that a day would come when life wouldn't be a struggle.

I wouldn't have made it through this part of my life if I didn't have the picture of Jesus holding me. I had gone through a vicious attack. Why would God let it happen? How could I be OK with it now? It's so simple that most won't believe me. God in His infinite wisdom gave man free will. As long as man has free will, there will be evil in the world. I do not hold any resentment against my attackers. I have forgiven them, as I needed to do that for my healing. Would I like an apology? Of course, but my future happiness doesn't depend on it or the actions of anyone. Did God let something bad happen to me? *Let* is an interesting word: to allow or permit meaning to give permission for. Did God give permission for this? Seriously? Did He allow it to happen? Really? I have heard it over and over again from people in emotional turmoil: How could God allow this to happen? To blame God for all the bad but ignore Him for anything good seems to be the norm in society. I prefer a God that allows free will, that doesn't make us robots to do exactly what He deems to do with us as it pleases Him. Because of that, there will always be pain in the world. **The question is more about what choices you are going to make with your free will.** Are you going to inflict pain upon others because you can? Will you choose to stay wounded and enclosed in the protective environment you have created? Or are you willing to risk experiencing life to the fullest, to find a place of wholeness, a place of peace?

Others may question why the attack was not stopped. I have already admitted to the fact that Jesus was with me. It was a question that I wrestled with. I didn't toss it aside just because I have found peace. I had much anger that I had to get past so that I could see the truths. With allowing free will, there cannot be choices about what you stop and what you don't. In my case, the attacker wasn't stopped. It was at the moment of my surrender, when there was no fight left in me. My attacker seemed to be resting to get ready to come to finish me off. It was at that very moment that I was led to safety. I was not followed. It was someone in a fit of rage like that, who wasn't likely to let me go, but I wasn't followed. Once I crawled away, the attack did stop. An attack that was certain to lead to death had indeed been stopped. As angry as I was as I was trying to heal, I also began to see that it wasn't God's plan for my life to end at this moment. It was a definite issue that I had to work through, and one that didn't go away overnight. I had to find a way to express my profound anger with God yet leave the relationship with Him intact.

I needed to find out what God's plan was in keeping me alive and allow Him to show me why I was still here. I wanted to stay angry, to walk away from Him screaming. What would that gain me? I had already seen that God had a better way for me to live. Why would I leave Him now? It was the hardest part of my healing: to not be angry at God, a God whose very character is love. My faith and belief in Him had to deepen. I had to reach in my deepest being to put aside my thoughts about the matter. It was only then that I could begin to receive all that God had to offer.

His offer was a life of purpose, a life that brings fulfillment and peace. I have found a place free from torment. I no longer need to be angry to push everyone away. I can find a place of refuge with God at every moment of every day. I know that He has my back, and that brings great comfort. Does that mean I don't believe I will have painful moments in my future? No, it only means that I know that with God, I can get through it. Maybe not standing, but possibly crawling. Still experiencing the heartache, but having the full knowledge that this is just a moment in time that will pass if I allow myself to let God work.

You can see it any way you want to. I prefer to see what God has been able to do through me and continue to do because of the healing He brought me through. Naïve? No. Faith. I understand the sovereignty of God. It doesn't mean I have to like it. It does require me to trust in Him. To trust in something that cannot be seen. So much of the world thinks that is nonsense. I have learned that to try to live in this world without Him is the crazy way.

Back to the nature versus nurture debate. Was I born the way I believed I was—as a man trapped in a woman's body? Or was it my surroundings and experiences? One could say that the attack forced me to turn my back on being a girl: something fragile and easily targeted for attack. The fact that I was triggered into a flashback when something quickly came into my vision on the left was easily explained; all of the blows were dealt to me by a right-handed assailant. I didn't become left-handed in response to it. It's a silly use of an analogy that you can blame on the debate. I did crave being in a closet every time I felt unsafe, maybe unknowingly searching for that voice that brought me to a place of healing. That was the craziest part of not having this active memory. I still wanted the safety of a closet. The older I got, the more I couldn't understand it. When I was in a disagreement with someone and it got heated, I wanted to go sit in a closet. Or when I lived alone and fear came in, the desire was to sleep in the closet. As the flashbacks came to stay, I even considered buying an air mattress that would fit the closet, but I never acted on those desires.

I have a hard time believing it was my experiences that caused my choices, as I had no recollection of those events. Maybe a better way of saying it is that it wasn't in my active memory bank. I have since been told that the body remembers. Once they were given a voice to heal, the repressed memories surfaced. The abuse could have subconsciously contributed, but then we are back to the undesirable debate, when in all reality, it really doesn't matter. I don't have a need to place blame somewhere. What happened to me shaped me into who I am today. Allowing the memories to come forth, to find a way to heal, all in order to bring me to the point of wholeness.

By following God and the path He laid out for me, I found a life worth living. One that I didn't have to mutilate my body to attain. I was willing to go to great lengths to find peace and contentment. Somewhere along the way, God stepped in and showed me a better way. It was never the easier way. **Nothing about my walk with God has ever been easy. Fulfilling and worthwhile, yes.** Did I want to quit and run away? Often. Where was I to go? For years, I dwelt on killing myself as the way to run away. I am so thankful that I never went that way. I am equally thankful that I pursued a life with God instead of a life that required time with a surgeon.

That may be a short-sighted statement, as I had to allow God to repair me, remove things that I had held onto that I never should have had, and accept the gifts that never should have been taken from me. Let me explain that in greater depth. I hope that repairing myself is self-explanatory. I was damaged goods. Just as I have taken my car to the shop for repairs, I had to allow myself to be overhauled by God. The release of anger was only accomplished as I allowed Him to show me the cause of it. I didn't always go willingly or quietly. Actually, I am certain it wasn't quietly. I was moaning and groaning all the way, only to find that I was a much happier person when I let my anger dissipate.

I was given so many things that God never intended a child to have. Shame being at the top of the list. Isn't it interesting that as a victim, I was the one who carried around the shame? *Shame* defined as the painful feeling arising from the consciousness of something dishonorable or improper. I didn't do anything wrong. I didn't deserve what happened to me, yet I was the one being held in bondage by shame. I was the one who believed that I was destined for a life as the target of abuse. Verbal, physical, and emotional abuse, and every subcategory you can come up with. It was years of having that ingrained into every ounce of my being. It was years of work for the belief to set in that none of that was true. I was loved, and I did deserve a life worth living.

What was taken from me included self-worth and childlike innocence, which resulted in the loss of my carefree childhood. I carried an underlying stress that a child isn't meant to have. I had a life of scrutinizing every moment, wondering if I was being deceived. What exactly was it that someone wanted from me? I was always questioning, never relaxed or confident in who I was. Peace was traded for survival. I had one best friend as a child. I couldn't stand it when something tried to come between us. I didn't believe she would stay my friend if she found something better. Looking back, I realize we were inseparable. She accepted me with all my anger and distrust. I never saw her faults, and she never saw mine. We were friends. Good friends.

Lessons Learned from Cupcake

I adopted a beautiful Persian kitty from a no-kill shelter. The name she had been given was Cupcake. I was certain that I would have to change her name, as I couldn't imagine having a pet named after food. The adoption process required a lot of lengthy paperwork. The entire time, Cupcake lay silent in the pet carrier. Once we were finally in the car, I was certain that she would begin to cry and be upset that she was trapped in the carrier. To my surprise, she didn't make a peep. She never lifted her head to look out the side, nor tried in any way to escape. If you have ever owned a cat, you are acutely aware that they think the world is coming to an end while they are trapped. Cupcake was a depressed, defeated, and motionless kitty. She was astutely aware that she was not in control of her circumstances. Her behavior saddened me. I couldn't imagine what this little kitty had been through that would cause her not to protest what was happening.

In order to slowly introduce her to her new home, I placed her in the bedroom and closed the door. I was delighted when I heard her pawing at the door, wanting out. As I started to push the door, she became frightened and ran to hide. I left the door open and returned to the living room to continue watching a movie. Within minutes, she was poking her head around the corner and scoping out where she was going to investigate first. Very softly, I said, "Hello Cupcake." She turned her head to look at me with wonderment in her eyes. You could tell she was surprised that I knew her name. I chuckled quietly at her surprise as I watched her slowly begin to explore. Unfortunately, any unexpected movement or sound sent her scampering to her hiding place. I never chased her, nor tried to find her place of refuge. I wanted her to have a safe place, somewhere she could go and be without fear: a place to calm her fears.

Being a Persian, she had a beautiful long coat of fur. In order to take proper care of her, I needed to brush her. The time came when I needed to attempt to hold her for grooming. Every time I picked up a brush, she ran for her safe place. Her fur was beginning to mat, and my concern was growing as to the mess she would be in if we didn't get her brushed. I felt I was in over my head, grasping at what could be done. I finally decided I would have to try to reach the name on the adoption papers to call with questions. I certainly obtained more information than I could have hoped for. My first question was about the brush that I should use. Imagine my surprise when I was told that Cupcake preferred to be shaved. A cat that didn't like her fur? I found out that the person I was talking to was the aunt, Jo, to the previous owner, and that I was Cupcake's third owner. Jo continued to fill me in, advising me that Cupcake was most likely abused by her first owner, and that her fur wasn't properly cared for. That they used the brush to pull through the fur mats. This most likely would have pulled the fur out by the roots, causing her intense pain. Why they gave her to the shelter is a mystery, but I'm glad the pretty girl escaped that life. As for her second owner, she had passed away from cancer, leaving Cupcake homeless. Once again, Cupcake was taken to the shelter, awaiting a possible new home. Life in the shelter meant the majority of her time was spent in a cage. She was given time each day to be out and about, but she spent her time on a shelf as high up as she could get. Away from everything else. A place where she wasn't bothered by another cat, and as far away as she could get from humans. Alone in her fear, depressed, waiting to be returned to her cage. By the time I had adopted her, she wasn't eating enough daily, and her weight had dropped significantly. The staff was thrilled that I was going to take her home.

After talking with Jo, I promptly made an appointment with a groomer. This turned into a traumatizing experience for both of us. I'm certain that she wasn't treated with proper care. Upon returning home, I had to start over to earn her trust again. Once again, the time arrived that her fur needed to be attended to again. I searched for a different groomer in hopes that it would be a better experience for her. This time she was treated with the love and the kindness that she deserved. This groomer enjoyed the challenge of shaving a kitty. This time, when we returned home, she ran from room to room with a happiness I had never seen. It was such a joy to watch her be free. As she paused in the living room, I said to her, "You like being naked, don't you"? I swear she shook her tail end at me in agreement and then ran off to jump with joy some more, knowing I wasn't going to brush her and bring her pain. I began to refer to her date with the groomer as her spa days. Her fur shaved, nails filed, and a pretty bow atop her head.

Shortly after Cupcake's adoption, my flashbacks were in full force, consuming my life. I soon realized that Cupcake and I were healing together. Just as I surprised Cupcake with knowing her name, I was learning that God had known me before one of my days came to be.[4] He knew my past even when I didn't know all that I had endured. Just as I had adopted Cupcake into my family and given her a place of refuge, I soon learned God had adopted me into His family and that He alone was my place of refuge. It was my choice how fast I pursued my healing. When it became too much, I withdrew into my place of safety. I lay in bed with the covers over my head or just sat in my home, ignoring the world that was going on outside the door. There were times of being on edge and not being able to handle any additional stimulation, and that was acceptable to God. He was always there, patiently waiting for me to seek Him when I was ready to move forward again. Just as Cupcake went from spending hours in her safe place to just minutes, I was able to go from days of hiding to a few hours. I still appreciate my alone time, but now it is a desired time instead of a time of hiding.

One day I was sitting in my chair, observing Cupcake's behavior. She would come into the living room, go behind the TV stand, to the far wall, then behind the couch, taking in every detail of what was going on to make sure it was safe to jump into my lap. I was amused by her behavior until I realized that I was behaving the exact same way with my Heavenly Father. His preference would be that my trust in Him would be so great that I would run for His lap and jump into His embrace. He wanted me not to have to make sure that everything was exactly as it should be before I slowly made my way into His lap. He is my Father—my pain is His pain. When I cry, He catches my tears and keeps them.[5] He doesn't want me to turn away from Him when I am not perfect. Seriously, if that was true, I would never run to Him. His arms are always open, awaiting my arrival. Just as I wish Cupcake would have not wandered around the perimeter of the room before allowing me time with her, my Heavenly Father wishes to have time with me. To bring my pain before Him, to cry with Him, and to find words of wisdom. Not to jump in His lap for approval, but to seek Him for comfort and peace, with the promise that He will always be found. I loved Cupcake, with all her unique quirks. I only wanted her to be able to be a kitty and enjoy the life of a pampered pet. I remember the day I caught her on video playing and was able to share it with Aunt Jo, only to discover that she had never seen her play before. Cupcake finally felt carefree enough to play. God was cheering me on to the day when I could run from room to room without the burdens that had been holding me down. To a time when my wounds would no longer go before me and interfere with important aspects of my life. A time where I would be free to live. A life where I would find fulfillment in ways that I could never have anticipated. Did Cupcake know what she was missing before the day she played freely? Doubtful. Did I know what life could be once I walked into a life full of freedom? Not a chance. I'm only grateful that God never abandoned me in the process. My healing came after Cupcake's short life ended. I didn't have nearly enough time with her, but the lessons I learned from her will always be with me. I needed that sweet kitty to love me as unconditionally as I loved her, and I needed us to walk together in finding what our lives were meant to be.

What Could Have Been

In writing my story, I have had an unexpected experience. I could tell you all the events and the wounds they caused. I couldn't have anticipated what would happen when I began to write them out after I had come to peace with everything, and put it all in a new light. I had spent a great deal of my life just trying to survive, not enjoying life, but holding on. Having to choose to live and not seek death. I wouldn't say that I was experiencing life to the fullest. I knew that life had been full of horrible things. Nothing good ever seemed to happen to me. I had settled because I didn't know differently. I was hemmed in by what I knew I could never do. For example, I was keenly aware that I would never handle dorm life, so college wasn't appealing. My fears dictated all of my actions. Wherever the waves of life threw me, that was where I landed. How could I plan a future when I didn't see one?

The saying is that if you fail to plan, then your plan is to fail. I had gotten to the point where I was afraid to plan. I couldn't handle failure any longer. Failure sent me to my safe place for days. It was best not to think that anything good could happen rather than to hope for it and be disappointed. I was sad, and I had accepted that I always would be.

During the process of writing this book, I began to see how much of my life was affected by things outside of my control. I then began to see what my life might have been if these events hadn't happened. I was angry at first, followed by a deep depression. My life had been wasted, spending so much time trying to find healing, yet I couldn't heal completely until the repressed memories came to light. Once they did, I certainly could not have handled dealing with them any faster than I did. The calendar rolled over and over as I sat, watching time go by and wondering if I could succeed in healing. I often thought it was too much to overcome. I tried to convince myself that I needed to learn to be content, yet I never stopped pressing on and choosing to at least continue to try. After all, what did I have to lose?

So here I am now, feeling healed enough to put my story on paper. Instead of finding joy, I found depression. I was finally free from the pain of the wounds, but now my mind started playing the what-if game. What if we had never moved from my small home-town? Leaving there took me away from the security of my best friend. I most likely would not have had to walk the hallways of school in fear. If that was the case, then my grades probably would not have dropped. With better grades in hand, would col-lege have been a consideration? Possibly knowing what I wanted to do in life? After much healing, I had come to the realization that I wasn't stupid. I had an ability to learn and was actually intelligent. It was very easy to fall into the trap of seeing that my life could have been different. The trap being that I was stuck behind circumstances that were beyond my control. Yet to be fair to myself, I needed to look beyond what I thought it would be like. To look realistically at who I was and who my friends became. My wounds were driving me. Could I have really come out of high school unscathed, fully functional, and successful? Sounds like a fairytale ending, doesn't it? It's so easy to think of what might have been, to see it as I wanted to see it. In actuality, I probably would have still found my way to alcohol and drugs, as the need for self-medication was real. A dead-end life in a small town, still without a hope of a decent future.

To look at the positive side of the move would mean allowing myself to find good. Not a familiar place for me, looking for the positive. The experiences that a bigger town afforded me, such as the additional friendships, were all priceless. To have a town to roam with my friends with fun activities. A bigger school with additional extracurricular activities. To have to compete to play in sports and not be given a position out of need. The school that I attended didn't appear to have an issue with bullies. My friendships were diverse, and there was not a classmate to dislike. It was an exceptional experience—one that I am grateful to have had. I found out a few years back that my friends tried to track me down for class reunions. It was wonderful news to hear. They missed me as much as I missed them. Oh, how I wish I could have finished high school here. How different my life would have been if I stayed there,

It is easy to see that life could have been different if I had spent more time in this place. Once again, my wounds were still with me. Haunting my mind, my behaviors. Could I have really excelled? Or is that my mind telling me that is how it would have gone? In truth, my grades had already begun to drop. Could I have pulled it together and brought them up? Or is moving on what kept those friendships so special? I hadn't turned into an uncaring, mean person. If I had stayed, would I have pushed them away as I did so readily in later years? Alas, we will never know. The next wave of my life came, and I was off to new adventures in a new city.

I adjusted to the first move with ease, but not the second. I never adjusted. In fact, I'm not sure I was ever allowed the chance to adjust. Hate towards me started on day one at the new school. Dad had befriended the neighbors, who had a daughter my age. She was kind enough to take me to the school to show me where my locker was and all my classrooms. She never gave me a second glance after she completed her favor to my dad. I understood her behavior. After all, she was gorgeous and ran with the popular crowd. I was certainly not material for the "in" crowd. I was an outcast from day one, and she knew it.

If we hadn't made this move, would I have decided that I would end my life on my 25th birthday? Would life have finally beaten me down to the point of stopping to live and only exist? That is a question that can never be answered with certainty. I believe that day would have come eventually. I was depressed at a young age. The depression was never addressed properly, as the world had not embraced mental health. There wasn't a way to address it properly, as there is today. Even if there had been, I cannot be certain that my parents would have taken the steps to get me help, nor would I have been willing to accept help. The fact is, I was unhappy with who I was. The fact is that I was convinced at this point that I was a man trapped inside a woman's body. Nothing was going to make me happy. Not a college education followed by a high-paying job. I didn't long to date the prom king or get married. If I had, would this have been enough to usher me into a life of bliss? Not likely. I was still haunted by my wounds, some of which were still hidden deep within my mind and yet to be uncovered. It was apparent to me that I had behaviors that I didn't understand. I'm not sure anyone on the outside looking in saw how deep they were. If they did it, they went unacknowledged and unspoken to me.

The easiest thing to have deep sorrow over was the lack of my parents making decisions for my life that brought about positive experiences. The lack of listening to my opinion was obvious. I was a pawn in their lives, destined to live out the results of their decisions. I had no say in where my life was headed. I believe this was one of the biggest factors in living a defeated life. It was obvious that they had little regard for me, which was the basis of my lack of regard for myself. Would life have been different if they had listened to me? My belief was that it would have been substantial. To be given a place to be heard, to be seen for who I was and embraced as such. My self-confidence would have surely been abundant. Would it? How can that be a sure thing?

In reality, could anyone understand me? I didn't have a full memory of what was guiding my thoughts and actions. I often left myself wondering why I had the behaviors I did. Even if the perfect person had been in my life to talk to, I do not believe I would have been ready for the repressed memory. It would have been too much to deal with at such a tender age. Believe it or not, it was best that I continue through life tossed to and fro by all of the different events. I had to mature and come to the place of realizing that I was driven to find a way to change. A way to find a life worth living. It couldn't have come in high school, or a couple of years after.

In talking about regrets, I must certainly address my years I spend cross-dressing. The time I spent with Grace was a time that some Christians would call an abomination. There was a time that I deeply regretted this part of my life. I had even made the statement that this was the worst mistake I ever made. To be completely honest with myself, I would have to say that these were the most important years in making me who I am today. Without Grace, I would have tried to take my life. If I was unsuccessful, I would have had repeated attempts. You can call my life with Grace an abomination; I would call it hitting bottom. I came to the realization that mutilating my body to make it appear male was not going to bring me the happiness and contentment that I longed for. Oh, how I wish all of that could have happened without Grace. In all honesty, it never would have. I felt her love for me, and it was a love I had never experienced before. How can I call that anything other than what it was? For me, it was amazing that I could be lovable. If I hadn't accepted Grace's love, would I have been able to accept God's? Some would like to argue that I was engaged in an unacceptable behavior, and therefore God had turned away from me. I think that is a short-sighted opinion. **I am God's child; my behavior may have grieved Him, but He loved still loved me. He loved me so much that He had something better for me.**

The question is, would I have let God into my life if I hadn't had my time with Grace? Would I have ever run out of options to find happiness if I hadn't tried to live as a man? If Grace had continued to stay with me, would I have had what I wanted? Would we go on to have a family? Would that have brought me contentment with life? That would be incredible, to think, "If all of that would have happened, life would have been perfect." The facts are still the facts; I had wounds that needed a voice in order to be healed. I never could have been a good husband or father. I'm certain it would have been another relationship that I would have walked away from, convinced that it would be better for everyone if I wasn't involved.

I am convinced that every experience I had in life molded me into who I am today. Without the hard knocks, would I have the empathy and compassion that I have for others now? If I had everything handed to me on a platter, would I have the ability to weather the storms of life, or would I crumble into a million pieces, never to be put together again? **To be able to embrace my past means to be free of it unconsciously or subconsciously affecting decisions for my future.** The scars are still there. It isn't as if I have forgotten everything. I can look at the scar and remember the pain that caused it. There was certainly a time when I believed the wounds would always be open and infected. To only see scars now is beyond my ability to explain. I am rarely at a loss for words. I am grateful to be where I am today: Whole. Healed.

Conclusion

As I was preparing to write this book, a friend asked me what the point I would want the reader to see would be. My initial thought brought me to a childhood nursery rhyme. Humpty Dumpty sat on a wall. Why was he on the wall? Did he put himself there, or was there more of a ledge that he was sitting on, contemplating his future? We are then informed that Humpty fell. How did he fall? Was he pushed? Many times, I felt like I was standing on the preverbal ledge, contemplating jumping off to end my life. Other times, I jumped blindly into following what I believed God was asking of me. When Humpty fell, he was broken into so many pieces that nobody, man nor horse, could put him back together. I seemingly was born into being a million separate pieces. Nothing fit together or went smoothly. You couldn't look at me and see a whole person. What you saw was someone who struggled with even the easiest aspects of life. One of my brothers once told me that he was afraid to talk to me because he didn't know what he would get in return. People saw me, but couldn't understand how to relate to me. Therefore, few even tried. It is my sincere hope that you have seen the million pieces I was and had a glimpse into my journey to wholeness. Man couldn't piece me back together again. God could and did.

As I began to yield my life to God, He took the million pieces and began to twist and turn them. Just as a child plays with a kaleidoscope, turning the tube to see all the pieces move into different positions. Each turn creates something beautiful, yet there is also a jostling of pieces as the picture changes. The masterpiece isn't ever finished, as the tube is turned and turned, creating something new each time. With God, the pieces moved continuously until they began to fall into place. Sometimes a piece had to be smoothed to make the edge connect with another piece. Some had to be trimmed, making them smaller than they were originally. Others had to be increased in size. Eventually the pieces fit together, creating something that was wonderful and beautiful.

I have walked the journey of following God to where I am today. I look back and cannot fully comprehend how I am where I am today. If you were to map out my journey as you would a cross country trip, using the starting point of Bangor, Maine, with the destination of wholeness in Los Angeles, California, the most direct route would be over 3,000 miles, or approximately 16 million feet. With my short stride, that still comes to 10 million steps, Most of us want to fly to arrive as quickly as possible. However, to allow God to fully do what He needed to do in me required a journey of walking next to Him. All that He asked of me was to get out of bed each day, embrace that day for what it held, and attempt to move forward. Some days I managed to go five steps, others maybe it was just one, and plenty of days I went backwards. Some days I could only lay prostrate before Him and cry. I may have felt I was laying in front of Him when in truth He was either holding me or lying next to me, telling me He would never leave me, and that He would see me through to the finish line. Then there were the days when I seemed to jump a mile ahead, leaping to the top of the mountain I had been climbing. I would stand there and take in the vastness of the territory that I had traveled, hoping that this was the destination that I had been searching for, only to look ahead and see another valley that I had to trudge through.

When I was child, sledding was a fun wintertime activity. I was full of anticipation as to what the trip down the hill would be. With anticipation, I would run and jump onto the sled to recklessly slide to the bottom, aiming for any obstacle that may cause me to fly through the air, not caring if the landing would be safe. The chore was dragging the sled back up the hill to do it over and over again. As an adult, standing atop a mountain only to realize that I had to go down in order to climb the next mountain did not contain the same excitement. It was disheartening to realize that I had not yet arrived. I would pull out my telescope to survey the land ahead, hoping that I could see the finish line. Although I wasn't sure what the finish line looked like, I still needed to look for it. I had to decide if I had it in me to keep going. I was trying to understand how much farther away it was and putting one foot in front of the other while holding on to hope that one day I would indeed know that I was whole.

The journey was tiring. The valleys were deep, and I often got stuck there. It took a toll on me and began to wear on those around me. The flashbacks had changed me. I lacked self-confidence before they started; now I was walking around a minefield, just waiting to be blown up over and over. I didn't have many who were willing to walk next to me. In fact, my pastors began to tell me that I would be happy elsewhere. It's true that I was just a shell of a human being when I was at church. I wasn't working on maintaining relationships; in fact, I avoided everyone when-ever possible. One of my fellow parishioners once told me that I was so holy for sitting in the front row for service. I laughed when responding, "I sit up here because nobody else will, and therefore I am left alone." A sad truth. I didn't want to be bothered by anyone. My mind was overwhelmed with tragic, pain-filled memories of a long time ago. To live in the present was too difficult, so I gave as little effort as possible in any situation I could.

Now I was faced with kindly being asked to leave my church home. This was the ultimate rejection that I had faced. I wasn't sure where to go, what to do next, or if I would even try another church. But God knew. A long time ago, He had placed those four women in my life. One of them, Nichole, was still an active friend. She had not only been a significant part of my journey, she was also invested in how it turned out. She convinced me to attend a new church that was starting up. Great, right? In a way, yes. It was incredible that Nichole wanted me with her. She wasn't done walking through the minefield with me.

The downside isn't as easy to explain. I hadn't been able to put the work into keeping a friendship alive and well. Now I needed to try to build new ones. There wasn't any common ground other than the church we attended together. To another, they were asking me simple questions to gain information about me. What they didn't realize was the effect their questions were having. Most of them were met with an awkward silence as my mind was processing the memories that had surfaced. The quick response that I wanted to give would have been like vomiting on someone. Nobody wants to be vomited on, nor did I want to do that, but the silence was equally terrifying. I had to go home and write out what I had been asked and what the response was in my mind. Then I had to pay to sit with my counselor, Courtney, to talk the memory back down and figure out what the appropriate answer would have been. My mind couldn't think basics any longer. Everything was arduous. Sigh.

It was here that I wanted to quit trying, but I had Nichole in my corner to remind me of just how far I had come and say that to give up now wouldn't serve me well. I knew I couldn't allow my feelings to control my actions. Instead I met with my new pastor to discuss the baggage I was carrying. He was incredibly supportive. He didn't keep me away from serving my church. He knew I still had something to offer, and he didn't withhold it from me. By serving, I was given an opportunity to build a foundation for relationships that didn't depend on my past. I could build on the common ground of what the church was doing as a whole, not me as an individual. I began to rebuild that inner circle of friendships that I could entrust my private struggles with. Not vomiting on them, but slowly bringing them into the horrors that I was trying to process.

Another mountain climbed without the finish line in sight. Seriously, how much more ground could there be to cover? Was my past really just too much to overcome? But now I had built a circle of friends that would encourage me to keep pressing on. What was most important to me was to be able to share without receiving either sympathy or rejection. I needed to put a voice to the struggle in a place of safety. All I asked in return was prayer. I didn't need the opinion of a person; I needed clarity on what God was asking me to do with the task at hand. As painful as it was, I knew I had to walk through it. There weren't any shortcuts left to try, nor could I put my head down and forge through. No, I had to take in the scenery, no matter how difficult that proved to be.

I reached a point where I felt stuck in a valley. The mountain ahead didn't have a landscape that was going to allow for easy passage to the top. Once again, I was disheartened. How could I have come so far to find a mountain that I absolutely couldn't climb or go around? Courtney suggested that maybe it was time to go backwards in order to go forward. Nope, not interested. Not interested for many reasons. The obvious one of not wanting to revisit my past, kicking up the dust that was on top of those tragic events. The other meant changing counselors. I was still being controlled by a fear of abandonment and rejection. Being sent somewhere else was not an option. If you are trying to get rid of me, then my preference is that you fire me as a client.

It was agreed upon that she would stay in my life in a limited role as I moved on to a more specialized form of counseling. In order to do this, I would be required to take the memories on in a direct fashion. There would be no generalizing it. The additional counselor I sought was specially trained for what I was about to do. It is called Eye Movement Desensitization Reprocessing Therapy (EMDR), which is a therapy that is primarily used to help individuals work through trauma. Keeping two counselors allowed me to have one who helped me continue to grow in my daily battle of overcoming the flashbacks. The three of us worked together in order to not have both counselors addressing the same area. EMDR focused on processing the traumas by revisiting them in a very organized and real manner. The EMDR sessions were insanely intense and draining. With Lauren's assistance, I began to revisit every aspect of the traumas. The torture, the beating, the being left for dead, plus several other wounds. In order to start, I had to tell her the best moments of my life, as well as the worst moments of my life. Yeah baby, sign me up for that! Fortunately, by now I was a seasoned client, well aware that what I was sharing would be held in the strictest confidence and was ultimately going to be for my benefit.

Somehow, I knew that if I could ascend this mountain before me, I would finally begin to be able to see the finish line. With great determination, I met with Lauren to take it all on. I wasn't going to shy away from the train wreck called my life. Nor was I going to stare at the bloody mess and be overcome by it. I didn't realize that I was unable to feel empathy for myself. After all, hadn't I gotten exactly what I deserved? In the middle of one of our marathon sessions, I could see that Lauren was holding back tears. She had the typical poker face that a counselor is trained to have, yet her heart was shining through her eyes in a way I could see. I couldn't feel what she obviously was. I wouldn't, as I was afraid it would engulf me, and I wouldn't come out of it. I asked her to share what she was feeling. She warned me that she would cry. I let her know that was OK. If she cried, then maybe I could feel something that would allow me to cry. She shared with me that she was crying for that sweet little girl, terribly abused, and terribly undeserving of that treatment. I wasn't able to cry or feel compassion and grief over what I had experienced as a little girl during that session, but by the end of our time together, I certainly had learned how to feel everything that I had suppressed for years. So much so that I often cursed her for bringing my emotions to life—all jokingly, of course. I had lived most of my life without healthy emotions, so much so that I had to learn how to process them in an appropriate way. This meant learning to be connected moment by moment, accepting what happened to me, and allowing my true emotions about it to be released … all the while trusting that God would be with me as I visited these new places in my heart. I had to not only process the feelings, but allow them to happen in the first place. To cry without hearing the threat, "I'll give you something to cry about."

I had to learn that crying was completely normal. In fact, crying allows one to feel grief, which in turn leads to being able to process it. Disappointing events in life deserve to be cried over. They deserve to be given a voice. All in a healthy way, so that they can be dealt with in order to move forward again. Stopping to grieve doesn't mean life stops; it just means that I have lost something and need to acknowledge it. I had lost the innocence of childhood. I needed to acknowledge and grieve it. I had accepted it, but now it was time to embrace it for what it was. It was an event that I didn't deserve. It was life-altering but didn't need to be in control of my future. I had to go find that little girl who I had hated my entire life. Where did I leave her? What would happen when I found her was not anything I could have anticipated. It's strange to explain that I really had left her behind, but when I opened that closet door to my memories, she was there waiting. Her face lit up and assured me that she was excited that I had come for her. As I embraced her, we became one. This is what I had been missing all my life. Together, we allowed God to walk us through the traumas, seeing each one for what it was. Accepting that it wasn't my fault that God had a place for me, a purpose. Nothing was going to stop that purpose from being fulfilled other than my lack of trying.

Knowing that God loved me was one thing. It only required that I accepted the words in the Bible to be true. After all Jesus loves me this I know for the Bible tells me so. Accepting that God loved me required much more. To not only allow myself to feel His embrace but to actually seek it out. That is a whole other process that I can't express in words. The main reason I can't express it is because I am not sure when or how it happened. As **I put my walls down, God slowly and gently came in. I have learned that nothing is too difficult for God.** I had to change my approach from whining, complaining, and expecting to asking, seeking, and knocking. Anticipating what God will do if I let him lead, showing me the path to take. Some may decide to put the label of Christian on me.

I can't argue with that, as I do believe in God, His Son, and Holy Spirit, but to me, it is much deeper than that. I am a follower of Christ, a disciple, going forth as He directs. Won't you be a fellow follower with me? Allow Him to bring you to wholeness and show you the purpose He has for you? Instead of looking at the reasons why you should follow Him, could you look at why not? What do you have to lose? I guarantee you have more to gain than you even realize.

For obvious reasons, I didn't use my girlfriend's real name. It is not for me to tell her story or even speculate on her actions. There were many names I could have assigned to her. I chose Grace, as I have learned over time that God's grace was always with me. I have done nothing to deserve all that He has given me, yet He has done more than I could ever capture in writing. Therefore, I find it appropriate to end this book with the lyrics from Amazing Grace.

Amazing grace, how sweet the sound
that saved a wretch like me.
I once was lost, but now am found.
Was blind but now I see.
'Twas grace that taught my heart to fear
and grace my fears relieved.
How precious did that grace appear
the hour I first believed.
Thro' many dangers, toils and snares I have already come;
'tis grace has brought me safe thus far
and grace will lead me home.

Home: the place of refuge in peace and wholeness.

References

1a) Isaiah 53 (NLT)

Yet it was our weaknesses he carried; it was our sorrows that weighed him down.

And we thought his troubles were a punishment from God, a punishment for his own sins!

But he was pierced for our rebellion, crushed for our sins.

He was beaten so we could be whole. He was whipped so we could be healed.

1b) Isaiah 53 (AMP)

But [in fact] He has bourne our griefs, and He has carried our sorrows and pains'

Yet we [ignorantly] assumed that He was stricken, struck down by God and degraded and humiliated [by Him].

But He was wounded for our transgressions, He was crushed for our wickedness [out sin, our injustice, our wrongdoing];

The punishment [required] for our well-being fell on Him, and by His stripes (wounds) we are healed.

2) Isaiah 55:8

"My thoughts are nothing like your thoughts," says the LORD. "And my ways are far beyond anything you could imagine.

3) www.mayoclinic.org

4) Psalm 139:16 (NLT)

You saw me before I was born. Every day of my life was recorded in your book. Every moment was laid out before a single day had passed.

5) Psalm 56:8

You keep track of all my sorrows. You have collected all my tears in your bottle. You have recorded each one in your book.

About the Author

Deanna was raised in the Midwest by a conservative family, moving eight times in twelve years. After such a transient experience, Deanna was unwilling to put down roots or allow long-term relationships. It was only after God became real to her that she settled down in the St. Louis area. Deanna has a passion to help others find their God-given identity and to provide hope to those who have been wounded that healing is possible for them.